Praise for *DIY Cocktails*

"This book gives the home bartender all the tools necessary to create amazing cocktails."

Mitchell Rosenthal, Chef/Owner, Town Hall, Salt House
and Anchor & Hope, San Francisco

"A quite clever, simplified DIY book for making cocktail recipes, with excellent information and variations for same, no less flavor charts, easy reference boxes for recipes, fine photography, and gag reels. Buy it, look it up; it's well worth the price."

Brian Rea, Legendary Bartender, Author,
and Former Bar Manager, 21 Club, NYC

"This book makes creating and mixing top-notch cocktails a snap."

Daniel Yaffe, Publisher, *Drink Me Magazine*

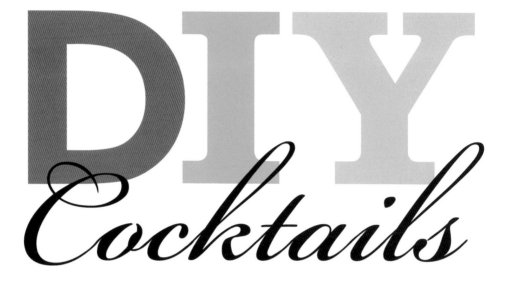

DIY
Cocktails

A SIMPLE GUIDE TO
CREATING YOUR OWN
SIGNATURE DRINKS

MARCIA SIMMONS & JONAS HALPREN, Editors of DrinkoftheWeek.com

Adamsmedia
Avon, Massachusetts

Published by
Adams Media, a division of F+W Media, Inc.
57 Littlefield Street, Avon, MA 02322. U.S.A.
www.adamsmedia.com

ISBN-10: 1-4405-0750-3
ISBN-13: 978-1-4405-0750-2
eISBN-10: 1-4405-1199-3
eISBN-13: 978-1-4405-1199-8

Printed in China

10   9   8   7   6   5   4   3   2   1

Library of Congress Cataloging-in-Publication Data
is available from the publisher.

This publication is designed to provide accurate and authoritative information with regard to the subject matter covered. It is sold with the understanding that the publisher is not engaged in rendering legal, accounting, or other professional advice. If legal advice or other expert assistance is required, the services of a competent professional person should be sought.
—From a *Declaration of Principles* jointly adopted by a Committee of the American Bar Association and a Committee of Publishers and Associations

Many of the designations used by manufacturers and sellers to distinguish their product are claimed as trademarks. Where those designations appear in this book and Adams Media was aware of a trademark claim, the designations have been printed with initial capital letters.

Readers are urged to take all appropriate precautions before undertaking any how-to task. Always read and follow instructions and safety warnings for all tools and materials, and call in a professional if the task stretches your abilities too far. Although every effort has been made to provide the best possible information in this book, neither the publisher nor the authors are responsible for accidents, injuries, or damage incurred as a result of tasks undertaken by readers. This book is not a substitute for professional services.

Photographs by Jackson Stakeman
Photo on page 15 © iStockphoto/MadCircles

This book is available at quantity discounts for bulk purchases.
For information, please call 1-800-289-0963.

For home mixologists everywhere with special thanks to our respective cats, who have been very patient about receiving less attention as we worked on this book

Acknowledgments

I can't thank Jackson Stakeman enough for taking such beautiful photos. His expertise and patience made the whole process a pleasure. Without the help of Jean Aw, I'm not sure how I would have survived finishing the book. She not only introduced me to Jackson and styled many of the shots but also opened up her home as a cocktail lab, photo location, and place to relax. Thank you, NOTCOT!

Thanks to my good friends, neighbors, and drinking buddies Joy Lanzendorfer and Kyle Rankin for introducing me to the fabulous world of fine cocktails and helping to inspire and test the ideas behind this book. I'm grateful that Jonas invited me to contribute to DrinkoftheWeek.com and embarked on this crazy adventure with me.

The work of the following people was extremely useful for research and inspiration: Dale DeGroff, Karen Page and Andrew Dornenburg, Michael Ruhlman, the Chow.com team, David Wondrich, and posters to Liqurious.com. (Also the late Harry Craddock and David Embury—and the book publishers who brought their work back to print.)

I am blessed to be surrounded by loving people who are excited about the work I do, and I thank all my family and friends for their support (especially you, Mom!). Special thanks to our agent, Kitty Cowles, and our editor, Victoria Sandbrook, for everything they've done for us.

—MARCIA SIMMONS

Acknowledgments

First, to Marcia, my partner in this endeavor, thank you for putting up with me. To Rachel for helping with cocktail creation and testing, and for putting up with me. To my brother for not drinking all the rye, and to my family for their support. To Kitty, for your guidance and belief in this project.

I would also like to thank all the mixologists who agreed to be interviewed and put up with my questions as you helped six other patrons. I'd also like to thank the giants (Dale, Tony, Brian Rea, you know who you are . . .) in the field who have never wavered from the mission to create fresh, terrific cocktails, even in the darkest of times. To Campari/SKYY and Pernod-Ricard for generously donating product for this project.

Finally, I'd like to thank the bartending community for the openness and camaraderie from which mixology has blossomed and is quickly regaining respect the world over.

—JONAS HALPREN

Contents

Introduction

Welcome to *DIY Cocktails*.

Why cocktails? In addition to being incredibly tasty, cocktails almost instantly impart a sense of community and togetherness. For us at DrinkoftheWeek.com, there is no greater way of bringing all of your friends together than throwing a cocktail party. In fact, cocktail parties were the inspiration for starting DrinkoftheWeek.com!

American history and cocktails are intertwined. The first cocktails sprang up in the American Northeast around 1800 and have been evolving ever since. The cocktail moved west and then abroad. But regardless of where the cocktail was served—in bars, saloons, lounges, clubs, pubs, and homes—it became the icon of neighborhood gathering places and instant brotherhood.

Until Prohibition, the American saloon keeper was a prominent member of society, and bartending was an honorable profession. The bartender not only served up amazing drinks but also provided entertainment and facilitated friendships. Unfortunately, Prohibition forced the best and brightest bartenders to flee to Europe since they were now outlaws at home.

As America emerged from Prohibition, it entered into the dark ages of mixology (a fancier term for bartending). With the best and brightest bartenders gone and no new generation trained to replace them, the secrets of the trade were lost. A few stars like Trader Vic led the immediate post-Prohibition era, but the end of Prohibition was followed by a descent into a prepackaged, processed, instant, artificial culinary world. And cocktails were one of the first casualties.

The artisan cocktail was lost for an entire generation. Growing up, so many of us knew nothing of smashes, frappes, highballs, and punches. Our experience was restricted by overpriced, under-spirited tropical cocktails made only with prepackaged ingredients. Home bartending was limited to mixing soda with spirit and ice . . . or maybe some drink mix.

Luckily, cocktails have emerged from the darkness. Mixologists are taking their place next to the world's top chefs, and bars are taking reservations. Fresh ingredients rule. Who could have imagined that only a few years ago?

We at DrinkoftheWeek.com have focused on the home bar. Creating an online center for bartending started as a hobby and turned into an obsession. We have vintage barware and cocktail books, and we sell better stock than most bars. Above all, we love mixing drinks and serving them to old and new friends.

We wrote this book to bring mixology magic into your home. This book is different. Rather than gathering a collection of recipes, DrinkoftheWeek.com aims to give you—the home mixologist—the tools to take your craft to the next level. In these pages we will show you the basics you need to get you started and share tips to ignite your inner bartender.

Cheers!

PART 1

The
Basics

Recipes, You're Not the Boss of Me!

1

Our mission is to help you make cocktails that taste good to you. But we haven't met you, so we have no idea what you like. That's why instead of giving you a book full of recipes you may or may not like, we're going to give you knowledge you can use to create *your own* recipes. Oh, and we're also going to give you a lot of recipes.

DIY—which stands for "do it yourself"—means making your own handcrafted, high-quality goods. While (hopefully) you don't consume cocktails in the same quantities you consume food, it helps to think of them in the same way. You probably don't eat all your meals in restaurants, and when you do cook at home, you probably don't use a recipe for every dish you make. DIY cooking is just a part of life. After years of cooking and eating, you have your own custom recipes for everyday life that cover a variety of occasions, styles, and tastes. You probably aren't frightened by making your own food, but the thought of creating a cocktail can

seem daunting. Our goal is to demystify home bartending so that mixing a drink becomes no more intimidating than making a sandwich.

We studied the classics and our own custom concoctions to find out what worked and what didn't—and from that we created fundamental cocktail ratios and the Flavor Profile Chart you can use as the building blocks for hundreds, maybe even thousands, of your own inventions!

Creating a new recipe comes down to choosing the ingredients, determining how much of each one to use, and knowing how to combine them. The possibilities are indeed infinite. However, the possibilities also fit into categories and ratios that make for perfectly flavored, perfectly balanced drinks. The crucial factor that distinguishes a perfect cocktail from a muddy mixture is the ratio—the simple proportions of one ingredient to another. The ratio of ingredients determines whether flavors that taste good together will mix harmoniously.

How a Cocktail Ratio Works

Instead of specific ingredients measured out in ounces, you'll see ingredient categories measured out in parts. A recipe tells you to mix two ounces of gin with one ounce of tonic; a ratio tells you to mix two parts of a "strong" ingredient with one part of a "weak" ingredient. (You'll learn about *strong, weak,* and the rest of the ingredient categories in a moment.)

Each part of a ratio represents a measurement. So a 3:2:1 ratio is simply telling you to put three measurements of one ingredient together with two measurements of another ingredient and one measurement of yet another ingredient. In Chapter 2, "Measuring," you'll learn the mechanics of turning a ratio with parts into a cocktail. First, you need to know how the ingredients you want to use—such as spirits, liqueurs, juices, and fruits—will be represented in the cocktail ratios in this book.

How We Categorize Ingredients

A ratio is just a set of numbers that stand in for your ingredients. You can't drink numbers, so it doesn't help you to know that a Tropical drink breaks down to a 4:3:1 ratio if you don't know what ingredients to use. Since you want to be able to use any ingredient you please, this book uses four broad categories to describe groups of ingredients: *strong, sweet, sour,* and *weak.* These four concepts form the backbone of traditional cocktail mixing. The Flavor Profile Chart in the Appendix takes a whole host of ingredients and fits them into one of these categories.

We used the following definitions to make sure you know *exactly* what type of ingredient this book calls for.

STRONG *Strong* refers to the spirits base of the drink—think gin, vodka, whiskey, and tequila.

SWEET *Sweet* ingredients are a form of sugar—be it simple syrup, liqueurs, or fresh fruit.

SOUR *Sour* flavors usually come from citrus, but with a little creativity you can also use tart fruits like cranberries. Aromatic ingredients such as aperitifs like vermouth and bitter liqueurs like amaro are included as a subcategory of *sour.* They are not at all interchangeable with sour fruits, so a section in Chapter 4, "Sour Power," specifies how to use them. Also check out the Flavor Profile Chart in the Appendix.

WEAK In this book, the word *weak* usually means water. Even if your cocktail doesn't contain club soda or tonic, there's still water in it. Shaking or stirring your drink with ice does more than chill it; it improves the balance with a bit of melted ice. In fact, a well-shaken cocktail will include about 25 percent water from melted ice. Ingredients like milk and cream are *mild* instead of *weak,* since they do not function in the same way as water and ice.

How This Book Works

The simple way to unleash your own cocktail creativity is to use proven ratios and adjust them to your taste. Knowing one cocktail ratio is like instantly knowing hundreds of drink recipes.

How does this work? Each chapter will show you:

- The fundamental cocktail ratio and its flagship cocktails: the classic and popular cocktails we think best demonstrate the ratio in action.
- Instructions for how to create your own cocktail using the proven ratio.
- A list of recommended ingredients and how they interact. You can substitute these ingredients into the flagship cocktails or use them as a guide when choosing your own ingredients for your custom creation.
- Sample recipes by the authors. For more inspiration, check out how we turned a simple ratio into a simply divine cocktail.
- Helpful sidebars that give advanced technique tips, advice on avoiding common mistakes, or recipes for our favorite handmade ingredients.

We're going to be bossy for a minute and tell you how to use this book. You don't have to read the chapters in order—although if you do, you'll notice that each chapter builds on information shared in a previous chapter. Here's our recommended approach:

STEP 1. Before making up your own drinks, try the flagship cocktail of the chapter to see how the ratio suits your taste. If you love it, go on to Step 2. If not, adjust the proportions slowly until it's perfect. Jot down that ratio, so you know how you might like to adjust other cocktails in the chapter. Everyone is different, so maybe instead of a 3:2:1 Margarita, you like a 2:2:1 or even a 2.9:2.3:0.8 Margarita.

STEP 2. If you're ready to design your own drink, consult the Flavor Profile Chart in the Appendix to see how the ingredients you've chosen will get along or to get ideas for flavor combinations. If you're still shy, follow one of our recipes to get the hang of this whole mixology business.

STEP 3. Taste each of your chosen ingredients separately to see how well you think they'll go together. Swap out or eliminate any that seem out of place. Then mix yourself a makeshift, teeny-weeny approximation of your cocktail. No need to whip out the shaker and ice—just taste all the final contenders together to make sure there's no unpleasant surprise.

STEP 4. Once you're fairly certain the ingredients will get along, mix away. Then taste your drink and, if necessary, make minor adjustments according to the instructions in the chapter. Remember that adding more liquor won't make your cocktail better, just stronger. Sounds logical, but a lot of expensive booze has been wasted trying to fix things that a squeeze of lime or a drop of bitters could have handled. We also encourage responsible drinking: Remember that a drink that is too strong can have consequences beyond tasting terrible.

STEP 5. Enjoy.

That last part is so important, we made it its own step!

Special Features

Along with the ratios and recipes you'll use as inspiration, this book has several features you can use to hone your mixology craft. **MIXOLOGY 101** sections will answer questions about cocktail basics—whether you're wondering whether to shake or stir or you're stumped about how to chill your drinks. **DIY GOURMET** introduces exciting flavors and new recipes for cocktail cornerstones including infusions, syrups, and liqueurs. **ADVANCED MIXOLOGY** delves further into bartending extremes—from a hard-to-find liqueur recipe to figuring out the alcohol content of your concoction. Other sidebars throughout the book will suggest fresh ingredients, warn you of bad combinations, and offer other tidbits you'll find helpful as you master the art of the cocktail.

What This Book Doesn't Do

Mixology has a lot of traditions and time-honored dictates most people don't care about. What matters is that your cocktail tastes good. We intentionally left out some information that, while important to professional bartenders, might confuse the average person. Anything requiring special equipment also didn't make it into the book. Every chapter is filled with techniques and recipes anyone can easily replicate in a typical kitchen. There are cocktails that don't fit into the patterns in this book, so those are not included either. But you'll find that learning how ingredients work together in our recommended proportions will give you skills, experience, and confidence to customize any recipe or formulate your own.

This book also won't give you recipes designed to cover up the taste of alcohol. The ratios in this book are inspired by the classic idea of creating a cocktail as a way to enhance spirits, and you will use fresh and homemade ingredients to complement liquor without obscuring its taste. Of course, if a drink is too strong for you or a guest, you can follow the tips at the end of each chapter for adjusting cocktails or create a whole new ratio based on our guidelines.

When it came to creating the ratios, we chose the proportions we think work best for the testing and tweaking inherent in designing an original cocktail. There are mixologists who recommend proportions for classic cocktails that are different from the proportions we've outlined in this book.

And you know what? Their drinks are probably amazing. But rather than confuse you with conflicting recipes, this book will arm you with a well-researched starting point to decide what *your* ideal cocktail is—not ours. Why? Because you should be able to *make* recipes, not just follow them.

Tools & Techniques Cheat Sheet

Cocktail experts are a passionate bunch with opinions stronger than 100-proof whiskey. Mixology advice often makes mixing a drink sound more intimidating than it should be: "If you shake a Martini, you'll bruise the gin" or "It's not a Daiquiri if you use simple syrup instead of sugar" or "If you don't use distilled water for the ice, your cocktail will self-destruct." This book won't insist that you use a particular type of glassware, brand of liquor, or mixing technique. After all, the goal is to teach you to make drinks *your* way. To make it easier for you, this chapter boils the complicated world of cocktail tools and techniques down to the basics so you can get right to concocting a perfect drink.

Glassware

The two most important questions to ask when choosing a glass for your cocktail are:

1. How big will my drink be?
2. Will my glass have ice cubes in it?

You can't serve a four-ounce cocktail in a two-ounce glass, so the reason for the first question is obvious. Aside from containing liquid, a glass should also help keep a cocktail cold. If you aren't using ice cubes in the drink, choose a glass with a stem. This way you won't heat up your cocktail by wrapping your hand around the glass. If ice cubes are keeping your cocktail cold, then you can use a stemless glass and wrap your warm palms around it with impunity.

There's special glassware for every spirit and cocktail, and the shape and size of a glass does affect the way you experience a drink. You might notice that some bars have just as many types of glasses as they do bottles of liquor. Practically speaking, most people can serve a wide variety of cocktails quite elegantly with only the following three types of glasses.

Highball or Collins Glasses

Both are tall and narrow. Highball glasses hold eight to ten ounces. Collins glasses usually hold ten to fourteen ounces. Aficionados will want both, but most people can do just fine with a set of ten- to twelve-ounce multipurpose glasses. Drinks served in these glasses typically contain ice.

how to chill a glass

Colder drinks taste better. Too much ice will dilute your drink, and some drinks don't contain ice at all. So serving cold drinks in cold glasses just makes sense. Depending on the cocktail scenario, you can use one of these three methods to chill your cocktail glasses.

1. Keep glasses in the fridge or freezer. This is the easiest method, but only if you have the room to do it. It works great for a small gathering or a quiet cocktail evening at home, but it isn't practical for a large party.
2. Fill glasses with ice and water. While you mix the drinks, fill the glassware with ice water and let them sit and chill. Dump the ice and water out and shake the glass just before you pour in your cocktail. This is a good method for medium-size parties with one bartender.
3. Keep glasses in ice. Make a little mountain of crushed ice. Turn the glasses upside down and store them in the ice. This is a good method for a large party or one where people are mixing their own drinks.

Old Fashioned Glasses

These four- to eight-ounce glasses are short and wide. They're sometimes called *rocks glasses* because they are used for serving drinks over ice, or *on the rocks.*

Cocktail Glasses

Also known as *Martini glasses,* these are cone-shaped with a stem and hold four to twelve ounces. Instead of Martini glasses, many hot spots are using *coupes*—four- to six-ounce shallow, rounded glasses with stems—and you could easily do the same. Usually cocktails served in either of these types of glasses are served *up,* or without ice.

Other Glasses

You'll probably want Champagne flutes, stemware for red and white wine, pint glasses, and shot glasses for your full-service home bar, depending on what you like to pour. If you want to geek out on specialty glasses, you can see a detailed chart of cocktail glass varieties at *www.drinkoftheweek .com/tools/glassware/.*

Bar Tools

Your kitchen is probably already equipped with paring knives, cutting boards, blenders, ice trays, strainers, measuring spoons, and measuring cups. Beyond these basics, there are a myriad of tools and gadgets just for bartending. Some will blow your mind; others will waste your cash. This section looks at the four specialized tools you simply can't make cocktails without.

Cocktail Shaker

The most common style is a *cobbler*—or *European*—*shaker*: a large metal or glass container topped with a built-in strainer and a cap. Bartenders rarely use a cobbler, favoring instead the *Boston shaker*: a mixing glass with a slightly larger metal container that slips tightly over the glass as a cover. With a Boston shaker, there are separate strainers that fit in the shaker. European shakers are easier to use, while Boston shakers are more versatile.

Measuring Shot Glass or Jigger

For most cocktails, you'll be measuring liquids in quantities that are smaller than a cup but greater than a tablespoon. A clear shot glass or miniature measuring cup is ideal for this. Cocktail experts usually recommend *jiggers,* which are two-sided measuring cups that look like hourglasses. These are convenient when you're making a lot of drinks very quickly because each cup represents a common measurement. For the average home bartender, a shot glass with markings is a more intuitive way to measure.

Cobbler

Muddler

This is a wooden pestle that looks like a miniature baseball bat. The flat end is used to smash ingredients, such as the lime and mint in a Mojito. We recommend wood because it won't damage your glasses. Some muddlers have teeth on the end, which is great for fruits but too hardcore for herbs. You can also make your own muddler; it's basically a wooden dowel.

Juice Extractor or Citrus Press

The inexpensive and easy way to get fresh citrus in your cocktails is to use a juice extractor or citrus press. If you want to get advanced, an electric juicer will do the job and then some; it can juice practically any fruit or vegetable.

Measuring

Normal people measure things in ounces, cups, tablespoons, and other recognizable increments. Cocktail people often use "parts" instead, which puts the recipe in the form of a ratio. A part can be any type of measurement. All you have to do is assign a measurement increment to be a part—for example, one part equals one ounce—then do a little bit of basic math.

Here's an example of a recipe given in parts:

Margarita

- ▸ 3 parts tequila
- ▸ 2 parts lime juice
- ▸ 1 part triple sec

To start with easy numbers, let's say each part is an ounce. In that case:

- 3 parts tequila would be 3 ounces.
- 2 parts lime juice would be 2 ounces.
- 1 part triple sec would be 1 ounce.

If you wanted to make a larger drink, you would use a larger part. For example, you could use that same recipe to make a pitcher of Margaritas by making one part equal half a cup. Or, if you wanted to serve your drinks in smaller glasses, you could make one part equal half an ounce.

Here's how that same recipe shown in parts would look in ounces if you decided one part was a half ounce:

Margarita

INGREDIENTS	RATIO
1½ ounces tequila	3 parts: ½ ounce × 3 = 1½ ounces
1 ounce lime juice	2 parts: ½ ounce × 2 = 1 ounce
½ ounce triple sec	1 part: ½ ounce × 1 = ½ ounce

Mixing Techniques

The method you use to mix your drink depends on the ingredients you use and the way you want your cocktail to taste. There are exceptions to every rule, but these guidelines work most of the time.

Shake

Shake cocktails that include fruit juice, dairy products, syrups, or thicker liqueurs so the ingredients can bond. Shaking with ice gives you a colder drink than stirring and imparts a little bit of water to the drink, which is desirable for cocktails like a Margarita, Sidecar, or Mai Tai. This is the most common method for mixing a drink, so shake when in doubt.

Fill your shaker most of the way with ice, and then add ingredients one at a time. For most drinks, shake vigorously for fifteen seconds before straining into your glass. If your cocktail includes thicker ingredients like cream or eggs, shake for at least thirty seconds. Don't shake bubbly ingredients like club soda, ginger ale, or Champagne.

Stir

Stir cocktails that consist of spirits and lightweight mixers like vermouth and bitters. Sometimes you'll stir the cocktail with ice but serve it straight up—like a Martini. Other times, you'll serve the drink over ice—like an Old Fashioned.

There are super-cool special pitchers and stirring rods just for this purpose, but you could do the same job with a topless shaker or mixing glass and a long bar spoon. Fill your container most of the way with ice, and then add ingredients one at a time. Stir your drink, and then strain out the ice when pouring.

Roll

Roll cocktails like a Bloody Mary that are made with purees or very thick juices. This prevents foaming. You'll need two glasses or a Boston shaker. Fill one glass or one side of the shaker with ice and your ingredients, and then pour the drink back and forth between the two glasses or sides of the shaker several times before straining the cocktail into your serving glass.

Build

Build cocktails like Cuba Libres or Moscow Mules that mix liquor with carbonated ingredients like ginger ale or soda. Fill half your glass with ice, pour in the liquor, and then pour in the mixer.

Preparing Ingredients

Certain ingredients or preparations come up over and over in cocktail mixing. Here's a quick guide to the ones you're likely to use the most.

Making Simple Syrup

Using simple syrup is an easy way to balance a cocktail with a little sweetness. Simple syrup can replace muddling a sugar cube and water in most cases.

Simple syrup

▸ 1 part sugar
▸ 1 part water

Combine sugar and water in a sealed container and shake it vigorously.

Superfine sugar (sometimes called *bartending sugar*) works best. If you're keeping the mixture for more than a week, add a tablespoon of vodka to preserve it, and store it in the fridge. Rock candy syrup, sometimes called *rich simple syrup,* is a mixture of two parts sugar and one part water. You'll occasionally see recipes that call for rock candy syrup because of its thicker texture and sweeter flavor.

Muddling

Muddling releases the oils from herbs and the juice from fruits. If you're muddling herbs—say you're making a Mint Julep—put the herbs at the bottom of a glass and press down gently with your muddler and twist rather than pound. Over-muddling herbs releases the bitterness from the stems, and you just want the flavored oil from the leaves. However, if you're muddling fruit or a sugar cube, go to town on that bad boy and smash away.

Rinsing

Sometimes you may want to add just a hint of a certain flavor without pouring the ingredient into your cocktail. For example, you may want a smidge of anisette or a touch of rosemary liqueur in the background. A Sazerac, which has an absinthe rinse, is the most famous cocktail that uses this technique. You can rinse by pouring a quarter ounce of your desired rinse into the serving glass, rolling it around to coat the glass, and discarding the excess liquid. (If you pour it back into the bottle, we won't tell.) If you have an atomizer or mister, you can spray the inside of the glass instead of rinsing.

Adding a Citrus Twist

When you hear someone order a cocktail "with a twist," what they are actually ordering is a little bit of citrus oil on top of their drink in the form of a strip of fruit zest. The flavor and aroma of the oil adds a little

complexity to dry drinks. You can make a twist from any kind of citrus, but lemon and orange are the most common.

To add a twist to any cocktail:

1. Cut the peel and a bit of pith in a strip about half an inch wide. A *citrus stripper* is a tool made especially for this job, but a paring knife or peeler can work just as well.
2. Hold the twist over the drink, colored side down, and twist it back and forth over the drink.
3. Rub the colored side of the twist over the rim of the glass and drop it into the cocktail.

Adding a Salt or Sugar Rim

Most drinks are rimmed with salt (like a Margarita) or sugar (like a Sidecar), but you can get creative and use things like cocoa powder, your own customized sugar, or a spiced salt. Adding a salt or sugar rim to the edge of your cocktail glass is simple:

1. Cut a slot into a wedge of citrus and put it on the rim. Squeeze gently as you rub it around the rim of

the glass to coat. Or pour a little simple syrup on a saucer, hold the glass upside down, and then dip the glass into the liquid to coat the rim.

2. Put the powder on a saucer. With the glass sideways, dab the rim in the powder as you slowly turn the glass. Only the outer edge should be covered. You do not want the powder in your drink.

3. Shake off excess powder.

Now that you've read through the basics, you're ready to move on to more delicious things. Before you dive into mixology, get to know your favorite spirits by tasting them straight and taking note of the flavors and aromas unique to each one. This will help you pair liquor with other ingredients, whether they be liqueur, syrup, or fresh produce. The first few chapters focus on complementing the unique characteristics of spirits. As the book goes on, you'll build toward cocktails that include a greater variety of ingredients. So grab a shaker and your favorite spirits; it's time to start mixing!

PART 2
The Ratios

The Original Cocktail

3

Maybe it's all the drinking, but bartending history is full of holes. Though we'll never really know when the Old Fashioned made its debut, the earliest known mention of it was in an 1806 publication. No matter when and where it was first mixed, this simple concoction demonstrates the difference between straight liquor and a cocktail. The Original Cocktail ratio is nine parts strong and one part sweet—topped off with two to three dashes of bitters. (To save you from figuring out how to measure .0008 parts, we kept the bitters in the traditional measurement of "dashes.") A sugar cube and a few drops of bitters transform how your taste buds perceive the spirit and bring out characteristics of the drink you may not have otherwise noticed.

Why It Works

An Old Fashioned uses bitters, sugar, and water to play with the characteristics of the liquor and enhance its flavor. The way something smells influences the way it tastes—just plug your nose while eating or drinking to find out how much. Before a spirit hits your tongue, its aroma hits your nose, so adding aromatic ingredients like bitters changes the way you experience your first whiff. For a brief moment, instead of smelling whiskey, you smell bitter herbs.

Sweetness is the perfect way to balance bitter flavors, and the sugar in an Old Fashioned brings out the sweet notes of whiskey. Add some large, slow-melting ice cubes, and you have a cocktail that opens up as you drink it. The citrus oil from an orange twist greets us just before the liquid finally touches your tongue.

This Ratio in Action: The Old Fashioned

RATIO 9 parts strong : 1 part sweet (with bitters)

Every bartender—home or professional—should know how to mix this classic. Although there's just a bit more than a teaspoon of non-liquor ingredients in this drink, the traditional recipe can still be translated into a ratio. First, let's look at a recipe expressed in exact measurements.

Old Fashioned Recipe

- 1½ ounces bourbon or rye whiskey
- 1 sugar cube
- 2 or 3 dashes of Angostura bitters

In an Old Fashioned glass, muddle the sugar cube and bitters, adding a bit of water to dissolve the sugar. Add ice, pour in whiskey, and stir. Garnish with an orange twist.

Here's the same recipe in the form of a ratio. Instead of a sugar cube with water, you will use simple syrup— something you learned about in Chapter 2, "Making Simple Syrup," that you'll revisit later in the chapter.

Old Fashioned Ratio

INGREDIENTS	RATIO
9 parts bourbon or rye whiskey	9 parts strong
1 part simple syrup	1 part sweet
2 dashes bitters for every teaspoon of sweet	

Follow the instructions for the Old Fashioned Recipe.

This ratio requires more math than the others in this book, so you may find it easier to reference the recipe before it when you're feeling less arithmetic-inclined—or if you've had a few already. No matter which method you use as a jumping off point for your libations, the result will be a well-balanced cocktail.

Customizing the Old Fashioned

If you get an Old Fashioned out on the town and see the bartender muddle orange slices and maraschino cherries as part of the mixing process, don't worry—the bartender didn't mishear your order. Mixologists are split on whether or not to include muddled fruit in this classic. We like it both ways! Rumor has it the fruit was added to the recipe during Prohibition to mask the harshness of bootleg spirits. However, today's smoother spirits still benefit from the addition of orange and cherry to this timeless tipple.

the ice is right

Whether it comes out of a dispenser in your fridge, a tray in your freezer, or a bag from the store, ice is an important part of mixing drinks. Throughout this book, you'd do just fine using standard ice cubes. However, the size and style of your ice does change your cocktail. Here are some things to note about your frozen water friend.

CLOUDY VS. CLEAR The reason why the ice you make at home is cloudy is because of minerals and impurities in your water. This isn't going to ruin your drink, but if you want clear ice, you *can* do it at home: Just boil distilled water and let it cool. Boil the water again. When it's slightly cooled, pour it into your tray and then freeze it. Either way, storing your ice in a closed container will keep it from picking up other flavors from the freezer.

TYPES OF ICE Melted ice is an ingredient in every cold cocktail. The smaller your ice cube (or square, sphere, or ring), the faster it melts. That's why you'll see bartenders serve certain whiskeys with a large ice square or ice ball instead of a group of smaller cubes. It's also why a lot of high-alcohol tropical drinks are served over crushed ice. Here's a breakdown of the most common types of ice:

- **ICE CUBES** are what you make in those freezer trays at home. Cubes are good for shaking or stirring, and they do a fine job in anything from an Old Fashioned to a Tom Collins. The optimal size for an ice cube is two inches by two inches—they fit in most glasses for easy stirring and don't melt as quickly as smaller cubes.
- **CRACKED ICE** is smaller than ice cubes. You make it by taking ice cubes, wrapping them in a clean tea towel, and hitting the towel with a mallet or hammer. The ice you buy in the store is usually cracked ice.
- **CRUSHED ICE** is even smaller than cracked ice and is great for high-octane, fruity drinks that can use the dilution by water. It's also great to pile on top of loose ingredients—like the mint in a Mojito—to keep them from going into your mouth or straw in mass quantities. ▸

the ice is right *cont'd*

- **BLOCK ICE** is what it sounds like—a huge block of ice. This is good for punches, since you want to keep them cold without watering them down too much.
- **ICE SPHERES**—which originated in Japan—are widely popular and perfect for a fine whiskey because they provide a slow supply of water. Many bartenders make these by hand from a larger cube. Lucky for us, molds are available so you can make nice spheres right in your freezer.

Here's the recipe:

(New) Old Fashioned

INGREDIENTS	RATIO
9 parts bourbon or rye whiskey	9 parts strong
I part simple syrup	I part sweet
I orange slice for every teaspoon of sweet	
I maraschino cherry for every teaspoon of sweet	
2 or 3 dashes bitters for every teaspoon of sweet	

Muddle the simple syrup, bitters, and fruit in the bottom of an Old Fashioned glass. Remove the fruit. Add the whiskey and ice, and then stir. *Optional:* Garnish with an orange slice and a maraschino cherry.

Some recipes say to top the (New) Old Fashioned cocktail off with some soda water. In Wisconsin, people drink their Old Fashioned with a little grapefruit soda.

Using a Different Spirit

As an American invention, the Old Fashioned was a showcase for American whiskey—which at the time of this cocktail's creation would have been either bourbon or rye. Tennessee whiskey wasn't widely distributed until the 1870s. But as the drink grew in popularity, an Old Fashioned starring other spirits became commonplace. David Embury, cocktail curmudgeon and author of the influential 1948 mixology masterwork *The Fine Art of Mixing Drinks*, mentions this gin version of the Old Fashioned with a funny name.

Stubby Collins

INGREDIENTS	RATIO
9 parts London dry gin	9 parts strong
1 part simple syrup	1 part sweet
2 dashes bitters for every teaspoon of sweet	

Pour the simple syrup and bitters into an Old Fashioned glass and stir with a bar spoon. Add ice, pour in gin, and then stir. *Optional:* Garnish with lemon twist.

You could easily make an Old Fashioned with scotch or Canadian whiskey, rum, tequila, brandy, apple-jack—the list goes on. Add infused spirits to your liquor cabinet, and the list of possibilities gets longer. Some store-bought infused spirits you could try in an Old Fashioned are:

- Red Stag black cherry bourbon
- Firefly sweet tea bourbon
- The Kraken dark spiced rum
- La Pinta pomegranate tequila
- Compass Box Orangerie orange-spice scotch whiskey

The Strong Stuff

An Old Fashioned is great for exploring how different spirits will perform in a cocktail. Any liquor goes well with sugar and bitters, although those ingredients best mirror the sweet and spicy notes of whiskey. You really can use any liquor, but here are the most traditional choices.

Rye Whiskey

Until Prohibition, rye was the most popular whiskey in the United States. Made with at least 51 percent rye, it's strong and slightly spicy, often with notes of cloves, cardamom, or pepper. For some reason, this spirit fell out of favor with American distillers after Prohibition—possibly because rye is more expensive than corn—and Canada flourished as the world's top rye producer. Now the United States is back in the rye business. And thanks to the resurgence of classic cocktails, rye has reclaimed its place in traditional drinks like the Old Fashioned.

Bourbon

This American whiskey is distilled primarily from corn and aged for at least two years in charred oak. Every brand is different, but in general, bourbon is lightly sweet—with notes of honey, maple, or brown sugar. It's a versatile spirit that pairs equally well with sweet, sour, and bitter flavors. Some bourbons pack a lot of heat, while others are more mellow. One thing they all have in common is an oak undertone.

Blended Scotch

Single malt scotch is often expensive and many reserve it for drinking straight or with ice or water. With a mild and faintly smoky flavor, blended scotch isn't quite as sweet as bourbon or quite as spicy as rye. This spirit is a bit more earthy—sometimes with a floral undertone.

Other Whiskeys

Irish, Canadian, and Japanese whiskeys are usually light-bodied and well-suited to mixing. They don't typically have smoke flavors and tend to be a little sweet. If you want something a little more mellow than bourbon or rye and less smoky than a scotch, these whiskeys could be your best choice.

Brandy

Brandy is made from distilling wine, which is of course made from grapes. Cognac, Armagnac, and pisco are types of brandy. Hints of oak and vanilla are common. There are also brandies distilled from fruits other than grapes—such as applejack or kirschwasser—although many of them could be too sweet for some Old Fashioned lovers' tastes.

Better with Bitters

Bitters are an alcoholic mixture infused with bitter or bittersweet ingredients. They're highly aromatic and serve to balance sweetness and cut a spirit's heat. In olden times, bitters were thought to be medicinal. So was whiskey, which means the cocktail may be even older than we think. There is an expanding market for artisan bitters, but the three most common ones are:

ANGOSTURA BITTERS This highly concentrated bitters preparation is the most well-known. When a recipe calls for bitters, it usually means Angostura bitters. The exact ingredients are a secret, but gentian root is the main bittering agent.

PEYCHAUD'S BITTERS While also made with gentian root, Peychaud's is lighter and sweeter than Angostura bitters. They are most often used as an ingredient in New Orleans' signature cocktail, the Sazerac.

ORANGE BITTERS Produced under several brand names—notably Regan's, Fee Brothers, and the Bitter Truth—orange bitters include orange peels, cardamom, coriander, and caraway seed.

There has been quite a bitters revival, so you can try more exotic varieties like grapefruit, cherry, chocolate molé, and celery bitters. If you're ambitious, you can even make your own. Check out the "Homemade Bitters" section later in this chapter for an easy recipe.

Good bitters and spirit pairings include:

- Cognac and cherry bitters
- London gin and grapefruit bitters
- Rum and Angostura bitters
- Vodka and just about any kind of bitters

We used orange bitters as the inspiration for a playful drink that shows off the versatility of the Original Cocktail.

Old Fashioned Fuzzy Navel

INGREDIENTS	RATIO
9 parts Peach Vodka	9 parts strong
1 part simple syrup	1 part sweet
2 dashes orange bitters	

Pour the simple syrup and bitters into an Old Fashioned glass and stir them with a bar spoon. Add ice, pour in vodka, and then stir. *Optional:* Garnish with an orange twist.

The Sweet Spot

Some bartenders use water and a sugar cube for the sweet part of this cocktail, and others use simple syrup. Since simple syrup is a mixture of sugar and water, it is essentially interchangeable with water and a sugar cube. Mixologists are split on which is best for an Old Fashioned. A sugar cube is the perfect measurement every time. We chose simple syrup not only because it's faster but also because it makes for a smoother drink. Bartenders used simple syrup as early as 1862, so don't worry that using it turns your Old Fashioned modern.

If you do want to modernize this classic, there are a lot of sweet ingredients out there besides sugar water. A spoonful of any of these sweets could change up this old standard:

- Fruit preserves
- Marmalade
- Agave syrup
- Maple syrup
- Flavored syrup

You may need to adjust the amount you use based on the sweetness of these ingredients. Here's a recipe that switches up the sweet:

El Moderno

El Moderno

INGREDIENTS	RATIO
9 parts reposado tequila	9 parts strong
I part agave syrup	I part sweet
3 dashes grapefruit bitters for every teaspoon of sweet	

Pour the agave syrup and bitters into an Old Fashioned glass and stir with a bar spoon. Add ice, pour in tequila, and then stir. *Optional:* Garnish with a slice of grapefruit.

If you can't find grapefruit bitters, orange bitters would also do a great job in this cocktail.

The agave syrup in this drink is a natural complement to tequila, which is an agave spirit.

Using Homemade Ingredients

Aside from muddling fruit into your Old Fashioned, there are other ways to add your own homemade flair to this cocktail. You can use:

- Home-infused spirits
- Homemade syrups or preserves
- Homemade bitters

Home-Infused Spirits

An easy way to enhance your DIY cocktail style is to use spirits infused with your favorite flavors. *Infusing spirits* means putting stuff in a jar, pouring liquor on top of it, and waiting for a day . . . or seven. Throughout the book, you'll find specific infusions to try out, but here are some general instructions you can use to infuse a spirit with any flavor you want.

Infused Spirit

▸ I part spirit of your choice
▸ I part flavoring item (herbs, chopped fruit or vegetables, or citrus rinds)

Put your flavoring item in a glass jar. Then pour in your spirit, seal the jar, and shake it. Let the infusion steep for one to seven days (length of time depends on how intensely flavored your ingredients are). Taste daily. Strain out the solids once the infusion has the desired flavor. Bottle and store as you would any other spirit.

Straining the finished spirit through cheesecloth can help make an infusion last longer because it will

Home-Infused Spirits

catch most of the small bits of fruit or vegetable that over time can start to change flavor inside the bottle. But if you plan to use your infusion within several days of making it, a fine-mesh strainer will work in most cases.

Vodka is the easiest spirit for infusing, because it pairs well with any flavor. But you can infuse any liquor you want. Consult the Flavor Profile Chart in the Appendix for ideas on which flavors and spirits are a good match.

We recommend:

- Cherry bourbon
- Basil vodka
- Cucumber gin
- Banana rum
- Orange-ginger tequila
- Peach-apricot whiskey

Because there's no set rule for how long to steep an infusion, each one will be different. An herb, for example, releases its flavors quickly, while more subtle ingredients like slices of pear take longer to impart its sweetness to the liquor. Recipes for infusions throughout this book give a suggested time-frame for steeping. The Advanced Mixology box in this chapter covers more information about how to estimate infusion times for your own, unique combinations.

Homemade Syrups or Preserves

If you're a home chef, you may already have syrup or preserves recipes you've used to take advantage of seasonal produce or your garden's bounty. That blueberry syrup or orange marmalade you made can do more than spruce up your pancakes. Chapter 5 depends heavily on homemade flavored syrup, but in the meantime, here is a homemade twist on the Original Cocktail ratio and a simple, flavored syrup recipe to go along with it.

Citrus Gin Jingle

INGREDIENTS	RATIO
9 parts London dry gin	9 parts strong
1 part lemon syrup*	1 part sweet
3 dashes orange bitters for every teaspoon of sweet	

Pour the lemon syrup and bitters into an Old Fashioned glass and stir with a bar spoon. Add ice, pour in gin, and then stir. *Optional:* Garnish with a lemon wedge.

Citrus Gin Jingle

*Lemon Syrup

- ▸ I part water
- ▸ I part sugar
- ▸ ½ part lemon zest

Bring water, sugar, and zest to a boil. Remove from heat and let the mixture cool. Strain out the solids and then refrigerate.

Remember how the Old Fashioned is made with muddled orange, maraschino cherry, and simple syrup? That mixture sounds a lot like marmalade—a fruit preserve made with citrus rinds. You can use a teaspoon of preserves with a little bitters instead of the muddled fruit and sugar.

Homemade Bitters

Making your own bitters often requires obscure ingredients and complicated techniques. You can order hard-to-find items online. If you want to experiment with your own, here are some things to keep in mind:

- Juniper, citrus rinds, cocoa nibs, or a bitter liqueur like Campari or Aperol can add the bitterness you need.
- A little goes a long way—a sprig of this or a few seeds of that can release a lot of flavor.
- High-proof spirits do the best job of extracting flavor from your ingredients.
- Long steeping times ensure the best result.

Even if you can't find angostura bark or gentian root, you can still make your own bitters. This recipe for DIY Cherry Bitters uses common ingredients you'll find at any grocery store. It's not as intense as Angostura bitters, but it adds dimension to your cocktail in a similar way. If you want more, just add another drop or use it in combination with stronger bitters.

more on infusing spirits

Making your own flavored liquor is something you play by ear—leaving herbs, fruits, or vegetables sitting in liquor until the infusion tastes right to you. To cut down the guesswork, here are some infusion tips.

PREPARING INGREDIENTS:

Herbs	Use them whole, including the stems.
Vegetables	Leave the skins on and then chop.
Citrus fruit	Slice thin or just use the zests.
Fruit with textured or tough skin, hard shells, or rinds (banana, pineapple, mango, kiwi, melons, etc.)	Remove and discard the skin or outer shell and then chop.
Fruit with soft skin (peach, plum, apple, etc.)	Leave the skins on, and then chop.
Berries	Remove greenery and leave whole.
Peppers	Cut in half or quarters.
Vanilla beans	Cut lengthwise.
Ginger	Peel and grate or slice thin.

ESTIMATING INFUSION TIMES:

Intense flavors	1 to 3 days	herbs, hot peppers, vanilla beans, citrus fruit
Moderate flavors	3 to 6 days	sweet melons, sweet peppers, berries, cherries, peaches, plums
Mild flavors	5 to 7 days	cucumbers, most vegetables, ginger, apples, pears, apricots

These are just general guidelines, and often we'll leave the mixture steeping for longer to make the flavor more intense. When combining flavors, you may want to remove the stronger flavor a day early to give the mellow flavor a chance to catch up.

DIY *Gourmet*
cherry bitters

Here's one of our favorite homemade bitters recipes:

- ▸ I vanilla bean, split lengthwise
- ▸ ¼ stalk lemon grass, cut into small pieces
- ▸ I star anise pod
- ▸ I juniper berry
- ▸ I clove
- ▸ I cardamom seed
- ▸ ¼ tsp. anise seeds
- ▸ ¼ cup dried cherries
- ▸ I cup rye whiskey

Combine all ingredients in an airtight glass jar. Seal and shake. Let ingredients steep for fourteen days, shaking once every other day. Then strain into bottle and store at room temperature. You can keep your homemade bitters for at least six months.

In the next chapter, we'll wow you with another simple bitters recipe, Sassy Red Bitters.

Ditch the Recipe— Use the Ratio

Now that you know how this seemingly simple cocktail can benefit from a little kitchen ingenuity, it's time to turn it into a new creation. Here's a recipe inspired by beautiful, bright-red cherries.

The Cheery Cherry

INGREDIENTS	RATIO
9 parts cherry infused bourbon	9 parts strong
I part simple syrup	I part sweet
3 dashes homemade cherry bitters for every teaspoon of sweet	

Pour the simple syrup and bitters into an Old Fashioned glass and stir with a bar spoon. Add ice, pour in bourbon, and then stir. *Optional:* Garnish with lemon twist.

How Did We Do That?

Beautiful, bright-red cherries inspired us to dream up this libation. Also, we wanted to show off our homemade bitters. As the Flavor Profile Chart in the Appendix shows, cherries and bourbon are BFFs—cherry can keep up with bourbon's sweetness while its tartness can add a little contrast. We were so pleased with all the cherry goodness that we didn't want to add any more fruit flavors in the sweet part of this ratio.

Let's take a look at what's at play in this newfangled relative of the Old Fashioned:

9 PARTS STRONG This is the cherry infused bourbon. Even though we added something sweet to the bourbon, it doesn't change the fact that our spirit is the strong part of this cocktail.

1 PART SWEET Simple syrup is the easiest, smoothest way to add sweetness to your mixed drink.

3 DASHES BITTERS You'll notice we used three dashes instead of two. We tasted this one and decided one more dash would push it over the top into greatness. It was fine with two, but we were aiming for perfection.

Your Turn

You can create your own Original Cocktail creation by asking yourself the same questions we did when making the Cheery Cherry.

- What ingredient or spirit do I want to feature?
- What flavor complements this spirit or ingredient?
- How do I want to use fresh ingredients? Infused spirit? As part of the sweet?
- What kind of bitters would draw out the flavors I want to emphasize and smooth out the sharper notes?

The Flavor Profile Chart in the Appendix will help you make the tough choices. There you'll find suggested flavor combinations, warnings for flavors that don't get along, and a quick rundown on a whole range of cocktail ingredients.

Adjusting Your Original Cocktail

Take a taste of your drink to see if it's all you dreamed it would be. (If you're making the drink for someone else, you can just dip a straw into the glass and place your finger over the top of the straw to grab some without

Homemade Bitters

drinking out of someone else's glass.) The ratio did a lot of the work, and now it's time for you to adjust it to your own preferences. Here's how you can get it just right:

TOO STRONG? Add a little sweet to taste along with a drop of water.

TOO SWEET? A dash of bitters can do a lot to balance out a cocktail that is too sweet.

TOO BITTER? Like yin and yang, a little sweetness can counteract the bitter.

TOO WEAK? This is the only reason to add more liquor to your cocktail—a stronger drink isn't always a better one. Add more spirits slowly and in small quantities.

RATIOS:

2 parts strong :
1 part aromatic sour, or
4 parts strong :
1 part aromatic sour

•

FLAGSHIP COCKTAILS:

Manhattan, Rob Roy,
Martini, Gibson

With a Dash,
a Splash,
or a Twist

4

Ask a few cocktail historians about the origin of the Manhattan and the Martini, and chances are you'll hear multiple stories. Both drinks (probably) appeared on the scene sometime in the 1870s. Like the Old Fashioned, they're proof that old-timey people sure liked high-octane cocktails. In the last chapter, we used the Original Cocktail ratio to experiment with strong and sweet—and your friend bitters—to change the way you experience spirits. The drinks in this chapter build on that knowledge, this time without using sugar. There are two ratios you'll be working with, both of which function the same way. You'll add a dash, a splash, or a twist to two parts strong plus one part aromatic sour or four parts strong plus one part aromatic sour. The term *sour* is very broad here because the way aromatic ingredients are used in this chapter has more in common with how you'd typically use a sour ingredient than a sweet one. This is your chance to top your drinks off with dashes, splashes, and twists of all sorts of ingredients, from bitters and herbal concoctions to onions and olives. Of course, you're also going to use fruits and homemade mixers that would have blown the minds of drinkers in the 1870s.

Why This Works

These simple-sounding drinks are actually quite complex. Aperitifs with herbal and bitter notes combine with the spirit to temper its heat and complement its primary flavors—such as oak in bourbon or agave in tequila—as well as draw out deeper characteristics like vanilla in Cognac or citrus in gin. A dash or two of bitters, a splash of another aperitif, some citrus oil, or a savory garnish is a minimalist way to complete your balancing act without complicating your cocktail.

In general, the two-to-one ratio works for liquors with a stronger, more intense character—like whiskey—while the four-to-one ratio works for clear spirits and more subtle flavors—like the botanicals in gin. This isn't a hard-and-fast rule. You can toy with a whiskey Martini or a vodka Manhattan, based on your own preferences. However, sticking to that rule of thumb could save you some failed experiments.

This Ratio in Action: The Manhattan

RATIO: 2 parts strong : 1 part aromatic sour

Purists will tell you a Manhattan should only be made with rye whiskey. While it's true that prior to Prohibition this was originally a rye cocktail, bourbon's sweeter character makes for an equally pleasant (some even say superior) Manhattan. Either way, what you're getting is a bold, balanced cocktail. Your garnish can accent the whiskey you choose.

Manhattan

INGREDIENTS	RATIO
2 parts rye whiskey or bourbon	2 parts strong
1 part sweet vermouth	1 part aromatic sour
1 or 2 dashes Angostura bitters	

Stir the whiskey, vermouth, and bitters with ice. Then strain into a chilled cocktail glass. *Optional:* Garnish with a maraschino cherry or a lemon twist.

Customizing the Manhattan

There are so many variations on a Manhattan that, if you're particular about your drinks, you should keep a close eye on your bartender when ordering this cocktail in bars. If you want to get playful with this drink at home, here are just a few of the ways you can monkey with your Manhattan:

MIX VERMOUTHS. Use ½ part sweet vermouth and ½ part dry vermouth rather than using 1 part sweet vermouth. This is known as a Perfect Manhattan. The word *perfect* here is just bartender-speak for half dry and half sweet vermouth and not a declaration of love on our part.

USE DIFFERENT BITTERS. Try orange, cherry, chocolate, or any other exciting flavor of bitters you can get your hands on. Add a splash of *amaro* or *amer*, an Italian bitter herb liqueur, instead of using Angostura bitters; doing that changes your Manhattan into a Monahan. Give Angostura bitters the boot in favor of a couple dashes of anisette, and you have a Narragansett. Why stop there? Maybe

Manhattan

you want to add a dash of absinthe or a splash of sambuca.

REPLACE THE BITTERS. Add a little touch of sweet to your cocktail with a dash of liqueur. Maraschino liqueur and amaretto sweeten it up while adding a little depth. Fruit liqueurs could be a nice counterbalance to the bitterness in some aperitifs.

CHANGE EVERYTHING BUT THE WHISKEY. If you replace the sweet vermouth with dry vermouth, skip the bitters, and add a splash each of maraschino liqueur and amer, your drink will be in a different borough. These changes make it a Brooklyn.

Using a Different Spirit

As an American cocktail, the Manhattan is traditionally made with American whiskey. But just swap in scotch, and you have another drink that your father (or grandfather) might have mixed up after a long day at the office.

Rob Roy

INGREDIENTS	RATIO
2 parts scotch	2 parts strong
I part sweet vermouth	I part aromatic sour
I or 2 dashes Angostura bitters	

Stir the scotch, vermouth, and bitters with ice. Then strain the mixture into a chilled cocktail glass. Garnish with a lemon twist.

You can also use rum or brandy instead of whiskey—both of which lend themselves to a splash of sweet or nutty liqueur instead of the bitters. Here's a recipe that gives a Caribbean twist to this vintage cocktail.

Island Manhattan

INGREDIENTS	RATIO
2 parts aged rhum agricole	2 parts strong
I part sweet vermouth	I part aromatic sour
2 dashes orange bitters	
Splash maraschino liqueur	

Stir the whiskey, vermouth, and bitters with ice. Then strain into a chilled cocktail glass. *Optional:* Garnish with a maraschino cherry or a lemon twist.

Infused spirits are a quick way to add more excitement to your Manhattan with little effort. Here are a few easy-to-find ones you may want to try:

- Firefly sweet tea bourbon
- Navan vanilla Cognac
- Seven Tiki spiced rum
- Leopold Bros. Georgia peach whiskey

To make the next cocktail, just replace the whiskey in a Manhattan with gin and skip the bitters. This drink is halfway between a Manhattan and a Martini.

Gin 'N' It

INGREDIENTS	RATIO
2 parts gin	2 parts strong
1 part sweet vermouth	1 part aromatic sour

Stir the gin and vermouth with ice, and then strain into a chilled cocktail glass. Garnish with a lemon twist.

The "It" in Gin 'N' It is sweet vermouth. So what happens if you ditch the sweet vermouth in favor of dry vermouth? Well, then what you have is a Martini—although one that is different from what modern drinkers are accustomed to.

MIXOLOGY 101
shaken or stirred?

You'll notice that when it comes to controversial cocktail questions, our stance is usually "Do whatever you like best." However, we feel strongly that the cocktails in this chapter should be stirred and not shaken. Shaking is great for combining ingredients of different consistencies or adding water dilution. However, the shards of ice, clouding, and light foaming that result from shaking don't do the drinks in this chapter any favors. You're mixing ingredients of equal heft, so stirring is sufficient to combine and chill them. Many bartenders shake away when making these cocktails, and if you want to do the same, we certainly won't (and can't) stop you. But we've found that stirring preserves the integrity of the spirits better, and these drinks are all about showing off high-quality spirits. (You'll find additional guidelines in Chapter 2, "Mixing Techniques" about when to shake and when to stir.)

Traditional Martini

INGREDIENTS	RATIO
2 parts gin	2 parts strong
1 part dry vermouth	1 part aromatic sour

Stir the gin and vermouth with ice, and then strain into a chilled cocktail glass. *Optional:* Garnish with a lemon twist, an olive, or nothing at all.

This Ratio in Action: The Martini

RATIO 4 parts strong : 1 part aromatic sour

Martinis started out with a modest proportion of gin to vermouth, but over time it became customary to use less and less vermouth. Supposedly, Winston Churchill took his Martinis with no vermouth at all—drinking chilled gin with a twist and bowing in the direction of France to acknowledge the source of the vermouth he was forgoing. The traditional recipe you learned earlier is smooth and fun to drink, although most Martini enthusiasts prefer a drier cocktail— that is, one with more gin. Make it with five parts gin for a Dry Martini or eight parts gin for an Extra Dry

Martini. For such a simple drink, there's quite a bit of disagreement about the ideal Martini ratio. After trying multiple variations, we think that all increments from two-to-one to eight-to-one are highly drinkable, but we agree with cocktail historian and author David Wondrich that the following recipe provides the perfect balance.

Martini (aka Dry Martini)

INGREDIENTS	RATIO
4 parts gin	4 parts strong
1 part dry vermouth	1 part aromatic sour

Stir the gin and vermouth with ice, and then strain into a chilled cocktail glass. *Optional:* Garnish with a lemon twist or an olive.

Customizing the Martini

The Martini inspires passion and controversy. Shaken or stirred? How much vermouth is too much? These basic questions can ignite arguments. No matter your exact definition of a Martini, you can't deny that it's a fun drink to play with. Make a few minor changes, and you have a whole new cocktail.

MIX VERMOUTHS. Just like with a Manhattan, using ½ part dry and ½ part sweet vermouth makes your drink what is called a Perfect Martini.

USE A DIFFERENT GARNISH. An olive or a lemon twist is the norm, but you can branch out. If you use cocktail onions instead, then suddenly it's a Gibson instead of a Martini. No reason you can't throw in a marinated cherry, pickled carrot, dried candied ginger, or anything else that floats your boat.

GET DIRTY. Turn your cocktails dirty by adding a little juice from the garnish container. A Dirty Martini results when you replace half the vermouth with olive brine. You don't have to stop there—cornichon, pickle, or cocktail onion brine; syrup from brandied apricots or cherries; or any other flavorful garnish drippings can transform your tipple.

ADD BITTERS. Early versions of the martini included bitters. Experiment with what a dash or two can do for you. Orange bitters pair well with a lemon twist. Celery bitters and an olive garnish make a good team. Bitters are also a good counterpoint to sweet vermouth.

SKIP THE VERMOUTH ALTOGETHER; USE ANOTHER SPIRIT INSTEAD. Add a splash of scotch to your gin and you have a Smoky Martini.

Using a Different Spirit

Go ahead: Join Team Gin or Team Vodka. Nothing is stopping you from switching teams at will. These two clear spirits are quite different, so whichever one you choose will change the character of your cocktail.

Using an infused spirit can add an extra punch of flavor to your cocktail. We recommend staying away from "flavored" spirits and sticking to those infused with real fruit.

Some interesting store-bought choices are:

- Square One cucumber vodka
- Boudier saffron gin
- Tru organic vanilla vodka
- Skyy Infusions ginger vodka
- Crop tomato vodka
- Seagram orange gin

Of course, you already know how to make your own infused spirits. Look back at Chapter 3, "Home-Infused Spirits," for a refresher on infusing basics or ahead to this chapter's "Home-Infused Spirits" section.

The Strong Stuff

Since you'll be topping off these drinks with a dash, a splash, or a twist, you have a lot of options for balancing flavors using small doses of powerful ingredients like bitters, herbal liqueur, citrus twists, and savory garnishes. So get adventurous with the spirits you choose! As you've seen so far, whiskeys, gin, and vodka will work great. Here are some other liquors we recommend.

Aged Rum

Darker rums that have been aged add sweet and layered flavors that are fun to pair with vermouth and other aromatics. It's an approachable spirit that gets along well with all manner of ingredients. Instead of (or in addition to) bitters, you may want to go with a splash of a sweeter ingredient to match rum's sweeter undertones.

Rhum Agricole

There are some finer points about where a spirit has to be distilled to be called *rhum agricole,* but generally speaking it's rum made from pure sugar cane juice instead of molasses. This was the common method in the French West Indies. It has a lower alcohol content than rum and is harder to find. The light-colored, less-aged version is the most common. However, the aged version provides a lovely herbal, fruity, and floral aroma and smooth mouthfeel that can really shake up your drink. Although it's pleasant, rhum agricole is a bit of an acquired taste because of its strong flavor.

Brandy

Cognac, Armagnac, and pisco are types of brandy—all made from grapes. Much like whiskey, many brandies are aged in oak and have a wide range of age classifications. Rich oak and vanilla notes are present, and the older a brandy is the more smooth and sweet it becomes. It has a thicker, almost oily mouthfeel compared with whiskey. Some brandies aren't aged, yet they are still extremely complex. Pisco is a good example.

DIY *Gourmet*
fig bourbon

Here's a recipe for one of our favorite bourbon infusions:

Fig Bourbon

- ▶ I part bourbon
- ▶ I part fresh mission figs, stemmed and quartered

Follow the instructions for Infused Spirit in Chapter 3, "Home-Infused Spirits." This recipe should steep for three to five days.

Sour Power, Aperitif Style

Sweet satisfies us and lingers on the palate, while sour stimulates us and cleanses the palate. Traditionally, aperitifs are served before meals to spark the appetite and prepare the tongue for new flavors. The word *aperitif* comes from the Latin *aperire*, meaning "to open," and when added to spirits, aperitifs do indeed open up the cocktail possibilities. We classify these aromatic ingredients as sour because their herbal—often bitter—flavors function in a similar way to sour ingredients by balancing sweetness. The drinks in this chapter aren't sweet in the same way sugar and fruit are, so the sweetness you're working with is in the form of undertones from barrel aging—like the honey notes in bourbon or the vanilla notes in Cognac. European aperitifs are hitting it big on the American cocktail scene, so there are a wide variety of options available to you. Many are identified with a particular brand name, while others come from a variety of sources. Here are just a few that work well in the types of cocktails you're playing with in this chapter.

Vermouth

Vermouth is fortified wine that's been infused with a mixture of herbs, water, and sugar. Some brands include Vya, Martini & Rossi, Noilly Prat,

Dolin, Punt e Mes, and Cinzano. Vermouth has a relatively short shelf life and will start to oxidize after opening. Store open vermouth in the fridge and it will stay fresh for up to a month. Any longer than that and you'll have some funky Martinis.

Sweet Vermouth (sometimes called Italian or red vermouth)

While we're juggling around words like *sweet* and *sour,* sweet vermouth doesn't actually taste sweet. However, it does have a higher sugar content and a less bitter taste than dry vermouth. It's a good complement to oaky, sweet spirits.

Dry Vermouth (sometimes called French or white vermouth)

Dry vermouth is sharp and slightly sour. It has a lower sugar content than sweet vermouth and a tiny bit more alcohol. It's a great match for botanical and neutral spirits.

Lillet Blanc

This wine-based aperitif is right in between sweet and dry vermouth on the dryness scale. It has more floral and citrus undertones, making it a great companion for botanical or neutral spirits.

Campari and Cynar

Campari is a bright-red, very bitter product made from herbs and aromatic plants. Reportedly it also is flavored with orange, rhubarb, and ginseng, though the company has kept the exact recipe a secret since 1860. Cynar is a similarly bitter concoction, only with artichoke in the place of fruit.

Playing with the Ratio: What If I Like It Tart?

If you replace the vermouth in a Martini with lime juice, what you get is a Gimlet—either the gin or vodka variety. There's juice involved, so these are shaken, not stirred. We normally wouldn't specify which brand to use or recommend store-bought juice over fresh; however, many mixologists insist on Rose's lime juice because it is sweetened and preserved, adding a unique flavor to the cocktail.

figuring out alcohol content

Here's a word problem for you: *There are two, five-ounce cocktails made with identical ingredients. The first cocktail is two parts liquor and one part nonalcoholic mixer. The second is four parts liquor and one part nonalcoholic mixer. In other words, the second one has twice as much liquor as the first. How much stronger is the second drink than the first?*

If you answered "twice as strong," you're wrong. The second drink only has 13 percent more liquor than the first. Let's plug in some ingredients and measurements to see why this is.

Cocktail No. 1

INGREDIENTS	VOLUME
2 parts vodka	= 3.33 ounces
1 part dry orange juice	= 1.67 ounces
Total before adding ice	= 5 ounces

The drink is about 67 percent vodka and 33 percent orange juice.

Cocktail No. 2

INGREDIENTS	VOLUME
4 parts vodka	= 4 ounces
1 part dry orange juice	= 1 ounce
Total before adding ice	= 5 ounces

The drink is about 80 percent vodka and 20 percent orange juice.

But all this tells you is how much liquor is in your drink compared with other ingredients. It doesn't actually tell you how strong your drink is or give you a clear idea of how intoxicated you might be after drinking it. That's determined by the percentage of alcohol by volume, or proof, of the spirits and other alcoholic ingredients in your cocktail. In general, the proof is two times the percentage of alcohol. So typical 80-proof vodka, for instance, is 40 percent alcohol.

If you'd like to get all mathy and figure out the alcohol content of your cocktails, check out this post to find out how: *www.drinkoftheweek.com/blog/how-to-calculate-the-alcohol-content-of-cocktails/*.

Alternately, you can add a splash of simple syrup to fresh lime juice in this sour classic.

Gimlet

INGREDIENTS	RATIO
4 parts London dry gin	4 parts strong
1 part Rose's lime juice *or* fresh lime juice with a splash of simple syrup	1 part sour

Pour all ingredients into a cocktail shaker with ice and shake for about fifteen seconds. Strain into a chilled cocktail glass. *Optional:* Garnish with a lime wedge.

For Splashing and Dashing

In Chapter 3, you learned about the benefits of bitters and a simple recipe for making your own. In addition to your old friend bitters, you can use herbal liqueurs for the same aromatic and balancing effect. Here are some beautiful aromatic liqueurs that would make a nice splash:

- Benedictine (multiple herbs)
- Anisette (anise)
- Galliano (anise, other herbs)
- Chartreuse (multiple herbs)

- Kummel (caraway, fennel, cumin)
- Ginger liqueur

You can even experiment with using these types of liqueurs in place of vermouth or other aperitifs in Manhattan- and Martini-style cocktails for a little added sweetness.

So far in this chapter we've made versions of this cocktail with different liquors but have stuck with either sweet or dry vermouth. You've already seen the Perfect Manhattan, which takes ½ part sweet vermouth and ½ part dry vermouth; together that makes one part sour for the ratio. Your recipe with two different sours would look like this:

RATIO	TOTAL
2 parts strong	2 parts strong
½ part sour	1 part sour
½ part sour	

This vintage recipe shows you another way to split up that part of the ratio with an ingredient that's drier and more bitter than dry vermouth.

The Valentino

INGREDIENTS	RATIO	TOTAL
2 parts gin	2 parts strong	2 parts strong
½ part sweet vermouth	½ part sour	
½ part Campari	½ part sour	1 part sour

Stir the gin, vermouth, and Campari with ice. Then strain into a chilled cocktail glass. Garnish with an orange twist.

Using Homemade Ingredients

It may not seem like there's much room to personalize cocktails built on the classic formulas for the Manhattan and the Martini, but there are four simple ways to add your own flair to this ratio:

- home-infused spirits
- home-infused aromatic sours
- homemade bitters
- homemade cocktail garnishes

Home-Infused Spirits

Thanks to the lessons in Chapter 3, you now know how to infuse spirits with any flavor you desire. Making them work with this ratio is a matter of choosing a flavor that pairs well with aromatics and then topping it off with the right splash, dash, or twist. Here are some combinations to try:

- Lavender-infused gin with dry vermouth, topped with a splash of Benedictine or an orange twist
- Chocolate-infused whiskey with sweet vermouth, and a dash of orange bitters
- Strawberry-infused tequila with amaro, and a grapefruit twist
- Cucumber-infused gin with dry vermouth, and a lemon twist
- Tomato-infused vodka with dry vermouth, and an olive

The next recipe features an unusual-tasting cocktail using a home infusion that takes almost no time at all. Most chocolate cocktails are sweet, but here we use bitter cacao nibs to bring in the tantalizing chocolate aroma without the sugar. Using a coconut-flavored rum as the base allows us a hint of sweetness to temper the intensity of the cacao. The bitters adds another layer to the cocktail—though the drink still tastes great without it.

Barbados

Barbados

INGREDIENTS	RATIO
2 parts chocolate-coconut rum*	2 parts strong
I part sweet vermouth	I part aromatic sour
I dash orange bitters	

Stir the rum, vermouth, and bitters with ice. Then strain into a chilled cocktail glass. *Optional:* Garnish with an orange twist or serve along with some dark chocolate.

*Chocolate-Coconut Rum

▸ 2 parts coconut rum

▸ I part cacao nibs

Follow the instructions for Infused Spirit in Chapter 3, "Home-Infused Spirits." This mixture should steep for one day.

Moving climate zones from Barbados to London, the new take on a Martini that follows is refreshing and light. Tomato is right at home with the garden flavors and scents in gin, calmed by the gentle presence of vermouth and a little Lillet.

Tomato Martini

INGREDIENTS	RATIO
4 parts tomato-infused gin*	4 parts strong
I part extra dry vermouth	I part aromatic sour
I dash Lillet Blanc	

Stir the gin, vermouth, and Lillet Blanc with ice. Then strain into a chilled cocktail glass. *Optional:* Garnish with a cherry tomato.

*Tomato-Infused Gin

▸ I part London dry gin

▸ I part ripe tomato

Follow the instructions for Infused Spirit in Chapter 3, "Home-Infused Spirits." When you strain out the tomatoes, press down gently. This mixture should steep for one to two days.

Home-Infused Aromatic Sours

By infusing wine or spirits with herbs, you can create your own home-infused aromatics. Without being an expert or using obscure herbs, you can concoct a decent facsimile that gives you the flexibility of including your favorite flavors and fresh ingredients.

Tomato Martini

Anise Super Star

The process is similar to making bitters. For the following recipe, we designed our own copy of anisette to bring the licorice scent and flavor of anise to our own creation. For our splash, we went with an Islay scotch to impart a unique, smoky touch.

Anise Super Star

INGREDIENTS	RATIO
4 parts vodka	4 parts strong
I part homemade anisette*	I part aromatic sour
I splash Islay scotch	

Stir the vodka, anisette, and scotch with ice, and then strain it into a chilled cocktail glass. *Optional:* Garnish with star anise.

*Homemade Anisette

- ▶ 2 tablespoons star anise, crushed
- ▶ I ½ cups vodka
- ▶ I ½ cups simple syrup

Combine the star anise and vodka in a glass jar and let steep for fourteen days. Strain and then add the simple syrup. Shake well and store as you would any liqueur.

Homemade Bitters

As you saw in the Chapter 3, "Better with Bitters" section, a world of ready-made bitters is available to you—anything from celery to chocolate has been commemorated in bitters form. You can even make your own bitters—like our cherry bitters recipe.

Campari is already bitter, so rather than hunting for hard-to-find bittering agents, we incorporated it into the following grapefruit bitters recipe. With fruit juice and sugar included, Sassy Red Bitters are mild and flexible—you can drop in a few dashes to top off a cocktail like the ones in this chapter or use it as a primary ingredient in another creation. The bittersweet flavor is a nice accompaniment to dry cocktails—you can even skip ahead and use it for the Champagne cocktails in Chapter 10.

The ginger in the bitters recipe inspired us to use the Sassy Red Bitters in a cocktail made with ginger liqueur. Since we're using a sweeter liqueur in place of the usual aromatics, this cocktail is less dry than the others in this chapter. But it's far from sweet, as the ginger adds a nice kick.

Sassy Bite

INGREDIENTS	RATIO
4 parts London dry gin	4 parts strong
1 part ginger liqueur	1 part aromatic sour
1 or 2 dashes Sassy Red Bitters*	

Stir the gin, ginger liqueur, and bitters with ice. Then strain into a chilled cocktail glass.
Optional: Garnish with a grapefruit twist.

Homemade Cocktail Garnishes

The maraschino cherry is many people's favorite part of a cocktail. You'll soon learn how to make your own, so why use the artificial, neon-red orbs you find in the grocery store?

The DIY Gourmet recipe for homemade cocktail onions will transform your Martini into a Gibson. If you're a Gibson guy or gal, don't count on mushy onions that have been sitting on the convenience store shelf for a

*Sassy Red Bitters

- ▸ 1 large Ruby Red grapefruit
- ▸ ⅓ cup sugar
- ▸ ½ cup water
- ▸ ½ tablespoon coarsely chopped fresh ginger
- ▸ 1¼ cups Campari
- ▸ ½ cup sweet vermouth
- ▸ 1 cup vodka

Cut the grapefruit in half. Juice one half and chop the other into large pieces. Cook the sugar and water over medium heat in a saucepan until it thickens (about three minutes). Then added the chopped grapefruit pieces and cook for an additional five minutes. Remove the pan from heat. Once the mixture is cool, pour it into a glass jar (including the grapefruit chunks) and add the remaining grapefruit juice, ginger, Campari, vermouth, and vodka. Shake the contents well. Let the mixture sit overnight before using. After two weeks, strain out the fruit to prolong the life of your bitters.

decade. The ones you make at home will be delicious.

You could always buy gourmet garnishes from specialty stores. But we don't recommend that when you can do it at home and control the quality and flavor without too much effort. Some DIY gourmet garnishes:

- **CANDIED CITRUS TWISTS** Coat lemon or orange rind sections in simple syrup and dip them in sugar. Bake at 150 degrees for thirty minutes, and then let them cool before use.
- **STUFFED OLIVES** Fill pitted green olives with roasted garlic cloves. Marinate them in the brine for at least a week so the flavors can marry.
- **LIQUEUR CHERRIES** Use our DIY Maraschino Cherries recipe, which follows, but choose a different liqueur, a different variety of cherries, or both. Bing cherries and bourbon-honey liqueur would be delicious, in or out of a cocktail.

DIY *Gourmet*
cocktail onions

Cocktail onions seem like an outdated garnish. A lot of bars don't even bother to stock them. However, when done right, they add a nice savory finish to a good stiff drink. Of course, you can't make a Gibson without them. Here's our recipe, which is as tasty as it is simple!

Herbed Cocktail Onions

- ¼ pound pearl onions, peeled
- 8 ounces Champagne vinegar
- ⅓ cup sugar
- ½ tablespoon salt
- ½ teaspoon pickling spices
- 1 sprig rosemary
- 2 basil leaves
- Splash of dry vermouth

Combine all ingredients except the onions in a saucepan and bring to a boil, stirring often. Reduce the heat and add the onions, simmering for about five minutes. Remove the pan from heat. Once it's cooled, pour the ingredients into a glass jar and add a splash of vermouth. Seal the jar and refrigerate overnight before using. These should keep for about two months.

There's no good reason why artificial, bright-red maraschino cherries are ubiquitous in bars and home refrigerators, since the homemade version is far better and is ridiculously simple to make. The hardest part is pitting the cherries, a boring but simple task easily pawned off on an unsuspecting significant other. Sour cherries most closely replicate the original maraschino cherries, but other varieties taste good, too.

DIY Maraschino Cherries

▶ 1 cup maraschino liqueur
▶ 1 pint sour cherries, pitted and stemmed

Simmer the maraschino liqueur in a small pot. Remove the pot from heat and add the cherries. After the mixture cools, pour it in a glass jar and refrigerate for forty-eight hours. The cherries should be good for at least two months.

Ditch the Recipe— Use the Ratio

It's time for adventure! The balanced 2:1 ratio and the drier 4:1 ratio both are a great starting point for experimentation. Using the DIY techniques you've just reviewed, we had some fun with each ratio to give you a better idea of what they can do.

Even if puns aren't your thing, you'll still have to agree that this deep-flavored take on a Manhattan is a lot of fun. Dubonnet and fig make for a sweeter drink without tasting sugary.

Hey, Fig Spender

INGREDIENTS	RATIO
2 parts fig-infused bourbon	4 parts strong
1 part Dubonnet	1 part aromatic sour
2 dashes homemade cherry bitters	

Stir the bourbon, Dubonnet, and bitters with ice. Then strain into a chilled cocktail glass.
Optional: Garnish with a maraschino cherry.

In this next Martini-style drink, lemon and basil unite with satisfying results.

DIY Maraschino Cherries

Lemon Basil Martini

INGREDIENTS	RATIO
4 parts lemon-infused vodka	2 parts strong
1 part Basil-Infused Dry Vermouth*	1 part aromatic sour

Stir the vodka and vermouth with ice and then strain into a chilled cocktail glass.
Optional: Top with a fresh basil leaf.

*Basil-Infused Dry Vermouth

▸ 8 ounces dry vermouth
▸ 1 fresh basil leaf

Follow instructions for Infused Spirit in Chapter 3, "Home-Infused Spirits." This mixture should steep for one day.

How Did We Do That?

We've been adding flavor to these drinks so far without any muddling or syrup making, and we're going to keep it that way. For the simple, elegant cocktails in this chapter, infusing is the best way to introduce flavors from the garden.

The 2-to-1: Hey, Fig Spender

2 PARTS STRONG With fig-infused bourbon, it was love at first sip. Figs have a rich, sweet flavor that is cut by a mild, almost apple-like tartness. The Hey, Fig Spender was our excuse to drink our fig bourbon as much as possible.

1 PART AROMATIC SOUR We chose to enhance the sweetness of the fig bourbon with Dubonnet, which tastes like a fruitier version of sweet vermouth, rather than fight against it with a dry or bitter aperitif.

AND A DASH To stop it from crossing the line from pleasantly sweet to overly sweet, we knew we'd need some bitters. Cherry and figs are great friends, as you'll see in the Flavor Profile Chart in the Appendix, so we reached for the DIY Cherry Bitters from Chapter 3, "Homemade Bitters."

The 4-to-1: Lemon Basil Martini

4 PARTS STRONG The tartness of lemon vodka was just what we need to give our sweet-smelling Martini a little kick in the pants. Topping it off with a basil leaf did more than make it pretty; it added a delicious aroma to prepare us for what we were about to drink.

I PART AROMATIC SOUR Sorry fenugreek, chervil, and cilantro—basil is our absolute favorite herb. It gives anything we make with it a fresh aroma and taste. We don't know why basil isn't as much of a cocktail standby as mint is, so we made it a featured player in our Martini variation. As an experiment, we dropped a leaf of it in some dry vermouth for a day to see what would happen. It let go of some of its entrancing scent and light herbal sweetness without changing the basic character of the vermouth. Perfect! Pretty much everything goes with basil. You could say it's the lemon of the herb world: No matter what you mix it with, it works.

Your Turn

By now you've been infusing away, and these Dash, Splash, or Twist ratios are another chance to let those infusions be the star of the show. And a recent rise in the popularity of European aperitifs and bitter herbal liqueurs has widened your cocktail horizons. When mixing with a dash, splash, or twist, just ask yourself the same questions we asked when creating the Hey, Fig Spender and the Lemon Basil Martini:

- What spirit do I want to use as a foundation for this cocktail?
- Do I want to infuse that spirit with a flavor? If so, which one?
- Does my spirit (whether infused or straight) have sweet undertones, or herbal and/or citrus undertones?
- Which aperitif best complements the undertone of my chosen spirit?
- Do I want to add another aperitif or herbal flavor?
- After tasting the cocktail, do I think it needs another herbal note, sweet note, or bitter note to balance it? Or would it be best served by a twist, olive, cherry, or other garnish?

These are strong cocktails, so you can't cover your mistakes with a lot of sugar or juice. To get an idea of how ingredients will balance each other, combine a teensy splash of each and taste before mixing. You'll be able to tell if they enhance each other or fight against each other. The Flavor Profile Chart in the Appendix has some more suggestions for you, so you won't be flying blind.

Adjusting Your Dash, Splash, or Twist Cocktail

Even though there aren't a ton of ingredients, this type of cocktail isn't too difficult to adjust if you're not completely happy with the results.

TOO STRONG? Before you get started, make a small drink to ensure you like the combination. If you've done that and still feel it's too strong, a splash of a sweet ingredient can make it more palatable. You can even add ice cubes for a little water dilution.

TOO SWEET? This could happen if your infused liquor has very sweet fruit in it or your splash of liqueur was bigger than you intended. Bitters to the rescue!

TOO BITTER? Some ingredients like Campari or amaro can take over if you use too much. A splash of another aperitif that is less bitter—or even a sweet ingredient like maraschino—can balance the bitterness.

TOO WEAK? This one's easy. Add a splash of liquor . . . but don't go overboard, because you can't take it back.

Playing with the Ratio: What If I Don't Like Bitter Flavors?

Sugar is good, and maybe after all these bitter flavors you kind of miss it. While future chapters will feature sweet ingredients, you don't have to skip ahead to find a cocktail that indulges your sugary needs. Here's a classic that is right at home with the manly mixtures in this chapter. Mint provides the aromatic accent!

Mint Julep

INGREDIENTS	RATIO
4 parts bourbon	4 parts strong
I part simple syrup	I part sweet
I sprig of mint	

Muddle one sprig of mint and simple syrup in the bottom of a shaker or mixing glass. Add the bourbon and then strain into a highball or double Old Fashioned glass filled with crushed ice. Stir gently. *Optional:* Garnish with a mint sprig.

This cocktail is a fun one to play around with. So many fruits go with bourbon, and you can smash them up along with your mint. Peaches, nectarines, blackberries, cherries, figs, and apples are just a few. And who says you have to use mint? Basil Juleps smell and taste just as good! You can even make a flavored syrup (see Chapter 5, "Homemade Flavored Syrup and Soda" to find out how) and use it in place of simple syrup to add fruit, vanilla, honey, or other flavors.

Notes

_____

_____

_____

_____

_____

_____

_____

_____

_____

_____

_____

Notes

Liquor Makes a Friend

5

The cocktails you've created so far have consisted almost entirely of a spirit—with hints of other flavors added to draw out and enhance the spirit's essence. Liquor did all the heavy lifting, so it's about time you let it have a friend. In this chapter, you'll explore two-ingredient cocktails as a jumping-off point for experimenting with more complex flavor combinations and ingredients.

The Liquor Makes a Friend ratio is the easiest one to remember: two parts strong and one part weak. Later in the chapter, you'll see you can use a 2:1 ratio to make cocktails that play with sweet and sour flavors. But you're going to spend most of your time on the version of the ratio that's used to make a Gin & Tonic—since it offers the most opportunity for experimenting with homemade ingredients.

Why It Works

You can tame any liquor's intensity—while still enriching its unique flavors—by pairing it with the right fizzy

water in the right proportion. Two parts strong and one part weak is a time-honored ratio because it ensures you're not watering down your drink, just giving it a boost. The refreshing bubbles and subtle flavors of tonic water or club soda literally lift your spirit—be it gin, vodka, or whiskey—and deliver it to your taste buds in small, bright bursts. When you make a Liquor Makes a Friend drink at home, you have an advantage over most bars: Individually packaged tonic water or club soda has better flavor and carbonation than the stuff bartenders get from a gun. Many high-end bars have started using individual bottles of tonic and soda in their cocktails.

This Ratio in Action: The Gin & Tonic

RATIO 2 parts strong : 1 part weak

You already know what's in a Gin & Tonic—the name of the drink also serves as its recipe. If you're drinking a Gin & Tonic, it's because you like gin and want to taste it.

Here are the proportions we think let the gin shine through:

Gin & Tonic

INGREDIENTS	RATIO
2 parts London dry gin	2 parts strong
I part tonic water	I part weak

Pour liquor into a highball glass filled with ice. Then add the water and stir. Garnish with a lime wedge.

The tonic water smoothes out the sharpness of the gin but has a little flavor of its own—thanks to a bitter compound known as *quinine*. Bonus: Quinine also makes drinks appear fluorescent under UV light, turning a Gin & Tonic into a liquid black-light poster. Rock on.

Customizing the Gin & Tonic

You don't need us to tell you that you can add fizzy water to liquor— Vodka & Tonic and Scotch & Soda are just two of the other Liquor Makes a Friend cocktails based on this concept. You can pair any liquor with a plain, sparkling friend. At the bar, you may have ordered a modified version of this cocktail with flavor-infused spirits, added a twist of citrus to the tonic water, or requested a flavored soda.

Here's an example of a simple twist on this classic:

Vodka & Tonic, Gingerly

INGREDIENTS	RATIO
2 parts ginger vodka	2 parts strong
I part lemon tonic	I part weak

Pour liquor into a highball glass filled with ice. Then add the water and stir. *Optional:* Garnish with a slice of candied ginger pierced through a lemon wedge on a toothpick.

Before you go all DIY on this basic cocktail, here are a few variations on this theme that you can make with commercial items:

- Absolut Pears vodka and tonic
- Gin and Stirrings Tart Cranberry club soda
- Bafferts mint gin and tonic
- Skyy Infusions passion fruit vodka and Fever Tree lemon tonic
- Jim Beam Red Stag black cherry bourbon and Boylan orange seltzer
- Gran Centenario Rosangel hibiscus tequila and tonic with a lime twist

Weak But Not Powerless

Weak is the classic cocktail term for ice and water—meant to contrast *strong,* the cocktail term for spirits. However, don't let the name fool you. Weak is no weakling. With only two ingredients in your drink, you need each one to do its job and do it right. So choosing bubbly water is not an unimportant job. We recommend you stock tonic water and club soda—both of which you can easily find under the Schweppes, Canada Dry, and Hansen's brands. Q Tonic, Fever Tree, and Boylan also make high-quality mixers,

though in some areas they may be harder to find.

At the grocery store, you'll see a whole shelf of fizzy waters with different names—tonic water, seltzer, club soda, sparkling water, and mineral water—and though the contents may look unsurprisingly similar, there are big differences between the varieties.

Tonic Water

Tonic water doesn't taste like water at all. Thanks to quinine, tonic water has a bitter flavor that makes it stand out from the other effervescent waters. The bitterness balances well with gin's strong herbal flavor. It also adds dimension to vodka, which has little flavor on its own. However, tonic water doesn't complement the sweet, woodsy notes of the brown liquors—which is why they are usually mixed with club soda instead.

Seltzer

Seltzer is just plain-old carbonated water with nothing added. You can use it interchangeably with club soda in drinks like Scotch & Soda or in

Fizzy Waters

more elaborate Collins- or Mojito-style drinks (see Chapter 10). If you make your own carbonated water at home using a gas charger or soda siphon, seltzer is the result.

Club Soda

Club soda is like seltzer, only with some minerals added for flavor. The difference is subtle, but the slight flavor boost intensifies the sweet qualities of aged liquors and fruits. For this reason, we prefer it over seltzer. It doesn't have the same bite as tonic water, so it doesn't add much to gin and vodka on its own.

Sparkling Water and Mineral Water

Sparkling and mineral water, like Perrier or San Pellegrino, contain naturally occurring minerals and can get their bubbles naturally or from forced carbonation. Neither of these are good for cocktails, because the minerals are too dominant and the carbonation levels aren't very consistent. Also, they tend to cost a lot more than tonic water, seltzer, or club soda without actually mixing well.

The Strong Stuff

The great thing about this ratio is that, in its basic form, you can use it with any spirit you want. (Well, you might make some aficionado's head explode if you poured soda water into a glass of thirty-year, single malt scotch or XO Cognac. For the record, we don't recommend you use those for mixing, but our heads will remain intact if you do.) Here's a quick look at liquors that have a happy friendship with carbonated water.

London Dry Gin

The rich bouquet of botanical flavors of gin really pop when paired with tonic. It's as if the two were made for each other. Every gin is unique—some gins will have a hint of cucumber, tea, citrus, or lavender in addition to gin's signature juniper flavor. Taste your gin straight and make note of the flavors so you can choose complementary flavors of your own to add to the weak part of this ratio.

Plymouth Gin

Lower in alcohol, Plymouth gin has an earthy flavor. Hailing from a single distillery in England, it makes a fine Gin & Tonic and mixes well with others.

Vodka

Often times, mixologists choose vodka because it plays well with the other flavors in cocktails. But vodka has some character of its own, and this is the ratio to show it. Tonic adds dimension to the astringency of vodka. Of course, vodka's friendliness allows us to try insane flavor combinations in the weak part of the ratio—with water and bubbles to regulate the intensity.

Tequila

All styles of tequila taste good in this kind of cocktail, but we especially recommend reposado and añejo—they've aged longer than blanco, or silver, and have more complex flavors. As long as you're using 100 percent agave tequila, it's hard to go wrong. Some tequilas have a hint of spice, while others play with a little sweetness. Either way, some refreshing tonic or a home-flavored soda is a fun

way to enhance the complex flavors you find.

Rum

Rum has a lot in common with tequila when it comes to using it in a Liquor Makes a Friend cocktail. All varieties of rum will work, but the darker aged rums—gold and dark—impart more character to a drink than white rum. Distilled from some form of sugar, rum will match well with the sweet flavorings you'll be mixing into your soda. Cachaca, a Brazilian rum-style spirit distilled from sugar cane juice, is another option.

Bourbon

The sweet nature of this spirit makes it an easy match for flavored soda. Some bourbons are stronger—or hotter—than others, but the oak aging imparts a distinct character. Most bourbon lovers would balk at mixing it with plain soda. However, the honey, vanilla, or brown sugar flavors present in so many bourbons pairs with a wide variety of fruits—and therefore a wild variety of fruit-flavored sodas.

Scotch

If you're going with plain soda water, this is your chance to use a scotch that might have more peat or smoke to it than would typically taste good in a mixed drink. Some blends, Speyside, and Lowland scotches are mild enough to handle some creative flavor matching. Taste your scotch on its own and pay attention to the nuanced effects it has on you. Do you taste citrus? What about pear or oak? Whatever you notice in there, use that to decide what other flavors to pair with your scotch—since the sheer variety in scotch makes it ill-advised to have a hard-and-fast rule.

Other Whiskey

Irish, Canadian, and Japanese whiskeys vary in sweetness and body—and they mix well. They don't use peat, so there is none of the smokiness of scotch. Approach these whiskeys like you would scotch: Taste first and then decide what flavor to complement.

Using Homemade Ingredients

If you have about five minutes, you can turn this simple cocktail into a showcase for your creativity. You can add any flavor you want to this simple drink in three ways:

- Use home-infused spirits.
- Mix homemade flavored syrup into your bubbly water.
- Do both.

Home-Infused Spirits

In Chapter 3, "Home-Infused Spirits," you learned how to infuse spirits with fruits, vegetables, and herbs. Infusing is as easy as chopping, pouring, shaking, and waiting. (Okay, so sometimes waiting isn't easy.)

Here are some flavor infusions we think would work well in this kind of cocktail:

- Cucumber gin with tonic water
- Vanilla vodka with tonic water
- Orange rum with tonic water
- Cherry bourbon with soda
- Strawberry tequila with soda

DIY *Gourmet*
apple-vanilla bourbon

Clear liquors aren't the only ones that you can infuse with fresh flavors. The sweet notes in bourbon make it a good match for apple and vanilla.

Apple-Vanilla Bourbon

▸ 1 cup bourbon
▸ 1 Granny Smith apple, cored and cut into chunks
▸ 1 vanilla bean, cut in half lengthwise

Follow the instructions for Infused Spirit in Chapter 3, "Home-Infused Spirits." The mixture should steep for three to five days.

We concocted the following recipe using home-infused liquor as the strong part of the ratio. We know what gin can do in this kind of drink . . . so what about giving tequila a chance to show off?

Blood Orange Tequila & Soda

INGREDIENTS	RATIO
2 parts blood orange–infused tequila*	2 parts strong
I part club soda	I part weak

Pour infused liquor into a highball glass filled with ice. Then add the soda and stir. *Optional:* Garnish with a blood orange wedge.

*Blood Orange–Infused Tequila

▸ 1 part silver tequila
▸ 1 part blood oranges, thinly sliced with peel and pith remaining

Follow the instructions for Infused Spirit in Chapter 3, "Home-Infused Spirits." This mixture should steep for three to four days.

Homemade Flavored Syrup and Soda

If you've ever had a Rum & Coke, you know that the effervescent part of this ratio doesn't have to sit there being plain. By adding a little syrup to your bubbly water, you can add a new flavor to your cocktail without a lot of work.

Some store-bought examples of syrups that can add character to your cocktail include:

- Torani black currant syrup
- DaVinci Tropical Fruit Innovations syrup
- Williams-Sonoma lemon-lime syrup
- Monin Wildberry syrup

But why buy when you can create a perfect syrup with just five minutes of work? Armed with the ability to make your own flavored syrup, you can turn a boring Vodka & Tonic into your own custom creation.

In Chapter 2, "Making Simple Syrup" you learned how to combine sugar and water as a replacement for a sugar cube. Flavored syrup is the same thing, only with an extra punch. Adding fresh fruit and herb flavors to your syrup is as simple as boiling water.

You may have already tried your hand at making lemon syrup for the Citrus Gin Jingle recipe in Chapter 3, but our Flavored Syrup recipe will serve for any flavor you want.

Flavored Syrup

- ▶ 1 part water
- ▶ 1 part sugar
- ▶ 1 part fresh ingredients (chopped fruits, sprigs of herbs, or a combination of the two)

Boil all ingredients for five minutes (or longer if you want a stronger flavor), let the mixture cool, strain out the solids, and refrigerate the liquid. About one quarter of the liquid evaporates in the cooking process.

The strained fruit makes a great topping for ice cream or cake! Note that while commercial syrups can last about six months, the homemade stuff lasts about three weeks. If you add one tablespoon of vodka for every two cups of homemade flavored syrup, the mixture will last up to two months.

Once you've made your own syrup, creating your own flavored soda water is just one simple step further. Just combine one part fizzy water with one part syrup.

Homemade Syrups

We used flavored soda water in the following recipe to add excitement to our vodka.

Black Rose

INGREDIENTS	RATIO
2 parts vodka	2 parts strong
I part blackberry-rosemary soda water*	I part weak

Pour vodka over ice in a highball glass. Then add soda and stir.

*Blackberry-Rosemary Soda Water

▸ I part club soda

▸ I part blackberry-rosemary syrup

First, follow the instructions for Flavored Syrup, using three-quarter part blackberries and one-quarter part rosemary. When the syrup is cool, stir it together with club soda. You can adjust the amount of syrup to suit your taste.

We chose club soda over tonic water because it has less flavor and we are already adding several flavors of our own.

Some other flavor combinations we'd recommend for your soda:

- Cranberry and orange zest
- Blueberry and lavender
- Kiwi and strawberry
- Raspberry and lemon verbena
- Lemon cucumber and cantaloupe
- Kumquat and ginger
- Lychee and raspberry
- Peach and cherry

Now your basic Vodka & Tonic isn't so basic anymore!

Using Infused Spirits and Flavored Soda

You know how to add excitement to your drink with home-infused spirits or DIY flavored sodas. Why not do both at the same time? Here are some wild creations you can mix up:

- Basil vodka and lemon-watermelon tonic
- Lime tequila and strawberry soda
- Pomegranate gin and lime-mint tonic
- Honey whiskey and cinnamon soda
- Tea-infused scotch and tamarind soda

Ditch the Recipe— Use the Ratio

Now it's time to let loose. You already know the proportion of strong to weak that you prefer, so it's time to use that knowledge to build the perfect cocktail. This is a chance to use your dream ingredient without holding back.

As we thought about this cocktail, crisp red and yellow bell peppers beckoned us from the produce aisle, so we answered their call. Here's what we created.

Bell Ringer

INGREDIENTS	RATIO
2 parts bell pepper–infused vodka*	2 parts strong
1 part honey-lemon soda**	1 part weak

Pour liquor into a highball glass filled with ice. Then add the water and stir. *Optional:* Garnish with a red bell pepper slice or a lemon wedge.

*Bell Pepper–Infused Vodka

▸ 1 part vodka
▸ 1 part red and yellow bell pepper, sliced thin with seeds discarded

Follow the instructions for Infused Spirit in Chapter 3, "Home-Infused Spirits." This mixture should steep for three days.

**Honey-Lemon Soda

▸ 1 part club soda
▸ 1 part honey-lemon syrup

Follow instructions for Flavored Syrup, using one part water, one part honey, and a half part lemon slices. When syrup is cool, stir it together with club soda.

How Did We Do That?

Bell peppers with honey and lemon doesn't sound at all related to the iconic, no-fuss Gin & Tonic. But a quick look at the steps we took will show how easy it is to go from basic to exotic.

Bell Ringer

2 PARTS STRONG Our bell pepper vodka is the strong part of this ratio. Infusing is a way to lightly incorporate unusual flavors. We wanted to feature something from the vegetable side of the produce aisle, so we picked up some red and yellow bell peppers. The green ones are a little more bitter, so we left them out of the bell pepper rainbow.

1 PART WEAK Club soda is our dependable friend when it comes to mixing up custom sparkling creations. We took a look at the Flavor Profile Chart in the Appendix and saw that honey and lemon complement each other and both give a little zip to bell pepper.

Your Turn

We started by simply adding blood oranges to a tequila and soda mixture. Then things got a little more complex with the Black Rose, which was inspired by a local fence full of blackberry vines next to bush after bush of rosemary. All this experimentation led us to the far more intricate Bell Ringer.

What all these drinks have in common is our decision to select what flavor or flavor group we wanted to play with. That's what you'll do, too. This ratio is so uncomplicated that you can unleash all sorts of crazy ideas on it with little effort.

Here are some questions to ask yourself when designing your own Liquor Makes a Friend cocktail:

- What liquor do I want to feature?
- What flavor goes well with that liquor?
- Will that flavor taste better married with the liquor or mixed with some sugar and added to carbonated water?
- Are there any other flavors I want to add?

The good thing about the homemade mixtures in this chapter is that they can be used in other cocktails or on their own—you can enjoy some home-infused liquors on the rocks or drink a fresh flavored soda instead of one from a can.

Adjusting Your Liquor Makes a Friend Cocktail

This ratio is easygoing—it will require little if any adjustment. Try a basic Gin & Tonic or Vodka & Tonic to see if you love our ratio or if you have a few tweaks to make. Then you can use that as your guide. If, after a little taste, you think your drink isn't quite perfect, here are some ways you can change that:

TOO STRONG? Spirits vary, and the one you use may pack more of a punch than you expected. You can add a little bit of plain tonic or club soda to cut the bite. If you used a flavored water, only add a little more flavoring syrup if you want it to be sweeter.

TOO SWEET? Sweetness isn't a big part of the original iteration of this drink, so it's possible that you can end up going a little overboard when adding new flavors. You can add more tonic or soda water if the sweetness is overpowering your drink. A squirt of lemon or lime may also balance things out.

TOO WEAK? This one is easy—just add a little more liquor.

Playing with the Ratio: What If I Don't Like It That Strong?

We chose two parts strong and one part weak because we like our cocktails with a little kick. However, lots of people love to flip that ratio: one part strong and two parts weak. Cocktails that have a greater proportion of nonalcoholic mixer than liquor are known as highballs.

You can make yourself a Gin & Tonic, Scotch & Soda, or any of the creations in this chapter using that inverted ratio for a refreshing and light cocktail. Add a little lemon or lime juice to that two-ingredient cocktail, and you've really opened up your options. (A Cuba Libre is a Rum & Coke with lime, for example.) Here's a recipe for the Moscow Mule, a classic highball.

Moscow Mule

INGREDIENTS	RATIO
1 part vodka	1 part strong
2 parts ginger beer	2 parts weak
1 lime wedge	

In a highball glass filled with ice, pour in the vodka and top off with ginger beer. Squeeze in the lime juice from the wedge. *Optional:* Garnish with a lime wheel.

Friend of a Friend

Liquor is friendly, so it's no surprise that you can turn the Liquor Makes a Friend ratio into all sorts of concoctions. The two-to-one proportion works well with different types of ingredients— not only strong and weak.

Strong + Sweet

Mixing liquor and liqueur is a big part of cocktailing—yes, we've decided *cocktail* can be a verb. Matching a spirit with a sweet liqueur is the first building block of creating a more complex cocktail, but it can also taste good on its own.

Here's a well-known, well-loved cocktail proving just that.

Black Russian

INGREDIENTS	RATIO
2 parts vodka	2 parts strong
1 part coffee liqueur	1 part sweet

Pour liquor into a highball glass filled with ice and stir.

Black Russian

Strong + Sour

Sour got jealous. By sweetening up your spirit, you can simply mix it with a sour for a quick-and-easy cocktail.

Whiskey Sour

INGREDIENTS	RATIO
2 parts whiskey	2 parts strong
1 part fresh sour mix*	1 part sour

Pour liquor into a highball glass filled with ice. Then add the sour mix and stir. *Optional:* Garnish with a lemon wheel.

*Fresh Sour Mix

- ▶ 1 part water
- ▶ 1 part sugar
- ▶ 2 parts lemon juice

Dissolve sugar in water to make simple syrup as directed in Chapter 2, "Making Simple Syrup." Combine simple syrup and lemon juice.

Cherry Stinger

INGREDIENTS	RATIO
2 parts cherry brandy	2 parts strong
1 part lemon juice	1 part sour

Pour liquor into a highball glass filled with ice and stir. *Optional:* Garnish with a lemon wheel.

Sweet + Sour

All this friend-making has made liquor tired, so it's taking a break. Put together sweet and sour, and you'll have a low-key, pleasant concoction.

Amaretto Sour

INGREDIENTS	RATIO
2 parts Amaretto	2 parts sweet
1 part lemon juice	1 part sour

Pour all ingredients into a cocktail shaker with ice and shake for about fifteen seconds. Strain into a chilled cocktail glass. *Optional:* Garnish with a maraschino cherry.

Midori Sour

INGREDIENTS	RATIO
2 parts Midori	2 parts sweet
1 part lemon juice	1 part sour

Pour all ingredients into a cocktail shaker with ice and shake for about fifteen seconds. Strain into a chilled cocktail glass. *Optional:* Garnish with a maraschino cherry.

RATIO:

3 parts strong : 2 parts
sweet : 1 part sour

•

FLAGSHIP COCKTAILS:

Margarita, Sidecar,
Cosmopolitan

Life of
the Party

6

Who'd have thought your most popular party guest would be a ratio? The Life of the Party has a strong personality but pays rapt attention to what others want. It's a popular, flexible ratio—sexy even. If you never look at another recipe book or remember another ratio, you can still be everyone's favorite bartender by using the Life of the Party ratio: three parts strong, two parts sweet, and one part sour. This is the backbone of favorites like the Margarita, Sidecar, and Cosmopolitan, as well as an easy starting point for concocting your own creations.

Why It Works

This cocktail is all about balance. Each element builds on the last without overpowering it. The Life of the Party Ratio is like a pyramid with a strong base, sweet center, and sour top. The strong part of the equation is liquor. This base spirit is *dry,* meaning it lacks sweetness. You want that dry, liquor flavor to shine through in your cocktail—just not quite as sharply as it does when served straight. So you'll add some *sweet*—enough to balance the dryness but not so much that you eliminate it entirely. Sweet is nice, but it's not very full on its own and can be overwhelming. Adding a little *sour* introduces some contrast and completes your balancing act. Now all your taste buds are happy!

This Ratio in Action: The Margarita

RATIO 3 parts strong : 2 parts sweet : 1 part sour

You don't walk into a bar and say, "Hey, bartender, I'll have a three, two, one." You'd just order a Margarita. Let's take a look at our favorite Margarita recipe so you can see this ratio in action.

Margarita

INGREDIENTS	RATIO
3 parts silver tequila	3 parts strong
2 parts triple sec	2 parts sweet
1 part lime juice	1 part sour

Pour all ingredients into a cocktail shaker with ice and shake for about fifteen seconds. Strain into a chilled cocktail glass. *Optional:* Rim the glass with salt and garnish with a lime wedge.

One reason we like this recipe is that it's in the middle of the dryness scale—meaning you taste the liquor more than you would in a Rum & Coke but less than you would in an Old Fashioned. Also, these proportions are easy to adjust by adding a splash more of any ingredient to taste. If it's not your ideal Margarita, it is so close that it doesn't take a lot of work to bump it up to perfection.

Customizing the Margarita

There are almost as many Margarita recipes as there are bartenders. Our favorite recipe is on the tart side, but with a little tweaking you can make a traditional Margarita that is a little sweeter. Here's how:

INSTEAD OF USING LIQUEUR, USE AGAVE NECTAR. Like tequila, it's made from the blue agave plant. If this gets too sweet for you, add a splash of water.

INSTEAD OF LIME JUICE, USE A MIXTURE OF EQUAL PARTS LIME AND ORANGE JUICE—or mix together one part simple syrup with one part lemon-and-lime juice mixture.

Triple sec is a liqueur flavored with bitter orange that's become the standard for Margaritas. Popular brands of triple sec include Hiram Walker, DeKuyper, Cointreau, and Grand Marnier. While similar, these vary in flavor since they are made with different base liquors and methods. Before you really start experimenting with what the Life of the Party ratio can do, it helps to see how simply substituting a different liqueur in place of triple sec will affect the Margarita. Just think of the other fruit flavors you could easily add by using another type of liqueur. Some other liqueur flavors you can try are:

- Raspberry
- Blackberry
- Peach
- Grapefruit
- Pineapple
- Tangerine
- Pomegranate
- Strawberry
- Apple
- Lychee
- Prickly pear

This list could be even longer, but fruit-flavored liqueurs are more popular for this drink.

Using a Different Spirit

Many cocktails were born because some bartender had the bright idea to mix in one spirit instead of another. Use brandy instead of tequila and lemon instead of lime, and that Margarita recipe turns into a Sidecar recipe. Brandy and tequila don't seem anything alike, yet they both taste fantastic in cocktails that are otherwise nearly identical. Here's a Sidecar recipe that uses Cognac.

Sidecar

INGREDIENTS	RATIO
3 parts Cognac	3 parts strong
2 parts triple sec	2 parts sweet
1 part lemon juice	1 part sour

Pour all ingredients into a cocktail shaker with ice and shake for about fifteen seconds. Strain into a chilled cocktail glass. *Optional:* Rim the glass with sugar and garnish with a lemon wedge.

Say you don't like brandy or tequila—what's stopping you from using rum? Nothing. In fact, that configuration is known as the XYZ Cocktail.

XYZ Cocktail

INGREDIENTS	RATIO
3 parts light rum	3 parts strong
2 parts triple sec	2 parts sweet
1 part lemon juice	1 part sour

Pour all ingredients into a cocktail shaker with ice and shake for about fifteen seconds. Strain into a chilled glass. *Optional:* Garnish with a maraschino cherry.

Substituting one liquor for another is just one way to expand your cocktail repertoire. The Margarita, Sidecar, and XYZ all taste different yet use the same ratio as the basis for balancing flavors and bringing out the best in the base liquor, or strong.

The Sweet Spot

So far these tried-and-true recipes have all used triple sec for sweetness. The flexibility and fun of the Life of the Party ratio lies in the sweet part of the ratio. This is where you devise your own flavor combinations and use fresh produce, like papayas, mangoes,

Sidecar

or raspberries. The sweet flavors come from liqueur, flavored syrup, and fresh fruit. There are three ways to use these sweets for a Life of the Party cocktail:

1. 2 parts liqueur
2. 1 part liqueur and 1 part sweet fruit juice
3. 1 part liqueur and 1 part flavored syrup

Think of liqueur as the vehicle for your other forms of sweet. Without it, your drink would have a thinner mouthfeel, the other sweet ingredients would have less to cling to, and you'd find yourself adjusting the sweet several times to get the right flavor and texture.

You can buy liqueurs, juices, and syrups—or you can make your own. For now, let's start by investigating how you will use liqueurs, juices, and syrups in your Life of the Party cocktails before continuing to other DIY projects.

Liqueur

Liqueur is basically sugar-sweetened liquor flavored with fruit, flowers, nuts, or herbs. You've already learned a simple way to customize a basic Margarita recipe—substituting a liqueur of your choice in place of triple sec. You can use this same concept to create a new Life of the Party cocktail using your favorite liqueur as the sweet part of the ratio. Liqueurs will vary in sweetness, so a handy way to judge a liqueur is to compare it side by side with your favorite triple sec to get an idea of how it will perform in your concoction.

Here are some liqueurs—including popular brand names you can find in the store—that taste great in Life of the Party cocktails:

- Chambord black raspberry
- Tamborine Mountain passion fruit
- PAMA pomegranate
- Bols wild strawberry
- LOFT organic tangerine
- Hiram Walker mango
- Leopold Brothers blackberry
- Midori melon
- Mathilde peach

Mixing Liqueur with Juice

A more advanced way to play with the sweet part of the Life of the Party ratio is to use a mixture of one part liqueur and one part fruit juice to combine for two parts sweet. Not only does this add another level of flavor to your cocktail, but it can also give you a way to balance very sweet liqueurs like Midori or to add more sweetness to an herbal liqueur.

Take a look at a familiar cocktail that uses this method in a very simple way.

Cosmopolitan

INGREDIENTS	RATIO	TOTAL
3 parts vodka	3 parts strong	3 parts strong
1 part triple sec	1 part sweet	2 parts sweet
1 part sweetened cranberry juice	1 part sweet	
1 part lime juice	1 part sour	1 part sour

Pour all ingredients into a cocktail shaker with ice and shake for about fifteen seconds. Strain into a chilled cocktail glass. *Optional:* Rim the glass with sugar and garnish with a lemon wedge.

Imagine simple variations on this cocktail—such as using black currant liqueur instead of triple sec and cranberry-raspberry juice instead of plain cranberry juice. You're simply splitting the two parts sweet portion into one liqueur and one part juice.

Here are some combinations of liqueur and juice that go well together:

- Limoncello and watermelon juice
- Fig liqueur and peach juice
- Amaretto and cherry juice
- Triple sec and grapefruit juice
- Cherry liqueur and raspberry juice
- Lavender liqueur and tangerine juice

Always mix together small, equal portions of your liqueur with your juice and taste them together before using them in a cocktail. This way you can make minor adjustments before you've added liquor or any other flavors.

We used this concept to design a drink that seems to have nothing in common with a Cosmo, even though they share the same skeleton.

Kentucky Apple Sour

Kentucky Apple Sour

INGREDIENTS	RATIO	TOTAL
3 parts bourbon	3 parts strong	3 parts strong
I part Grand Marnier	I part sweet	2 parts sweet
I part apple juice	I part sweet	
I part lemon juice	I part sour	I part sour

Pour all ingredients into a cocktail shaker with ice and shake for about fifteen seconds. Strain into a chilled cocktail glass.

Mixing Liqueur and Syrup

Using one part liqueur and one part flavored syrup for the sweet part of the Life of the Party ratio is yet another way to customize your cocktail. This works the same way as the liqueur and juice combination you just saw in action in the Cosmopolitan. Syrup is thicker and sweeter than juice, which you have to take into consideration when mixing it with your liqueur.

You can buy prepared syrup, such as those by Stirrings, Williams-Sonoma, or Torani, or you can make your own—which you learned how to do in Chapter 5, "Homemade Flavored Syrup and Soda." This is an opportunity to use some fresh ingredients that aren't totally sweet on their own—like pomegranate or kiwi—for the sweet part of your Life of the Party cocktail. It's also your chance to use fruits like figs or pears that aren't very cooperative when it comes to juicing.

Here's a cocktail we created using this method:

Mango-Berry Bash

INGREDIENTS	RATIO	TOTAL
3 parts gold rum	3 parts strong	3 parts strong
I part strawberry liqueur	I part sweet	2 parts sweet
I part mango syrup*	I part sweet	
I part lemon juice	I part sour	I part sour

Pour all ingredients into a cocktail shaker with ice and shake for about fifteen seconds. Strain into a chilled cocktail glass. *Optional:* Rim glass with sugar and garnish with a strawberry slice.

*Mango Syrup

▸ I part water

▸ I part sugar

▸ I part peeled and chopped mango

Follow the instructions for Flavored Syrup in Chapter 5, "Homemade Flavored Syrups and Sodas."

Experimenting with liqueurs, syrups, and fresh fruit is the most creative—and most difficult—part of concocting a Life of the Party cocktail. But it's not the only part. The two other elements of your cocktail, strong and sour, are just as important.

The Strong Stuff

It's not a cocktail without liquor, so you'll need to know how to choose the spirit that will be the star of your Life of the Party creation. Before you pick a base spirit, experience what each one tastes like on its own. Every brand will taste different from the next, but there are some basic characteristics that define a particular spirit. Let's take a minute to consider the liquors we think are particularly suited to the Life of the Party ratio.

Vodka

This spirit is friends with everyone, which makes it an experimenter's dream liquor. Because vodka has very little flavor of its own, it adds dryness to your drink without overpowering the flavor combinations you've chosen. Try it with kiwi, cilantro, or other flavors that can clash with more complicated liquors such as whiskey or brandy.

Light Rum

Also known as white rum, this liquor has more of its own flavor than vodka but still goes well with a wide variety of ingredients. It's particularly well-suited to tropical fruits, berries, mint, and citrus. Light rum has a little bit of sweetness, so it can also go surprisingly well with maple syrup and pumpkin—which both have a hint of bitterness. You can also use a gold or dark rum, but they aren't as versatile as a light rum in this ratio.

Silver Tequila

Make sure your tequila is 100 percent agave to get the true tequila taste—a light pepper-and-grass touch. Silver tequila lacks sweetness but has a slightly savory, earthy note. Tequila and citrus are best friends, but it also mixes really well with melon, pomegranate, prickly pear, watermelon, and berries. As with rum, you can go with tequila's darker counterparts if you account for their stronger flavor.

Brandy

Hints of oak and sweetness make brandy a wonderful companion for apricot, cherry, pears, all citrus, and figs. It clashes with non-citrus acidic fruits like kiwi and more savory flavors like herbs and salt. Apricot- and cherry-flavored brandies can complement simple cocktails.

Bourbon

Like brandy, bourbon is slightly sweet and oaky. Add to that a hint of rich honey, and it's a great accompaniment for apples, pears, peaches, figs, cherry, vanilla, mint, and citrus. Keep it away from more savory herb flavors, ginger, and watery sweets like cucumber and watermelon.

Gin

Think of gin as a fantastic but opinionated friend who will probably offend some of your more delicate party guests. Gin's strong juniper and botanical notes make it a little more challenging to mix with many of the sweet, fruity flavors recommended for Life of the Party cocktails. If you love gin and like a challenge, do a little trial and error to determine which liqueurs pair well with your gin. There are many classic cocktails that use gin and this ratio. To use gin in a Life of the Party cocktail, you just have to find sweets that pair well with powerful herbal flavors. We did, and here's what we came up with.

London Pomegranate

INGREDIENTS	RATIO
3 parts London dry gin	3 parts strong
2 parts pomegranate liqueur	2 parts sweet
1 part grapefruit juice	1 part sour

Pour all ingredients into a cocktail shaker with ice and shake for about fifteen seconds. Strain into a chilled glass.

Sour Power

Even though it is the smallest part of your cocktail, the sour is extremely important. Without it, you would not be able to achieve the balance and contrast that makes Life of the Party cocktails such crowd pleasers. Citrus is the optimal sour, since the acidity

brings out the best in a wide variety of flavors. You are safe using any citrus in a Life of the Party cocktail. As your flavor combinations in the sweet category become more complex, you will be better off sticking with something simple like dependable lime juice.

However, there's definitely room for a little creativity with sours. Unsweetened blueberry, pomegranate, and cranberry juice are sour. You may still want to add a twist of citrus to make them pop.

Playing with the Ratio: What If My Sour Isn't Sour?

It's possible to skip the citrus without making an overly sweet cocktail. Not every fruit falls squarely in the sweet or sour camp. Blueberries, for instance, hover somewhere in between. To bring out both the sweet and sour sides of these favorite berries, we muddled them with simple syrup and lime.

Blue Lychee

INGREDIENTS	RATIO
1½ ounces light rum	3 parts strong
1 ounce lychee liqueur	2 parts sweet
½ ounce simple syrup with a squirt of lime	1 part sour substitute
7 or 8 fresh blueberries	

Muddle blueberries in the simple syrup and lime juice in a mixing glass. Add rum, lychee liqueur, and ice. Top with the metal half of a Boston shaker (or transfer all into a European shaker) and shake for fifteen to twenty seconds. Strain with a julep strainer (or the top of your European shaker) into a chilled Collins glass filled with ice. *Optional:* Garnish with a lime wedge.

Using Homemade Ingredients

Now that you know how different types of ingredients work in Life of the Party cocktails, it's time to learn how to create homemade versions using your favorite produce.

Fresh Fruit Juice

The juice aisle of your supermarket has all sorts of flavors you can use in your Life of the Party cocktail. But when you make your own juice, you can take advantage of seasonal produce and create your own flavor combinations. You can juice certain fruits like oranges by hand. In most cases, however, you'll be whipping out your juicer, blender, or food processor to use your favorite produce. If you have an electric juicer, just throw your chosen fruit in and out comes juice. If you don't have a juicer, follow these three steps instead:

1. Peel and chop your fruit, removing any pits or large seeds.
2. Blend until smooth. This usually takes a minute or two.
3. Pour the mixture through a fine strainer, pushing down on solids.

This works perfectly for juicy fruits like pineapples and melon, but it doesn't work for very fibrous fruits like apples and bananas. (There are other ways to include those fruits in Life of the Party cocktails.)

When juicing and pureeing, stick with soft, juicy fruits. Adding a couple pinches of fresh mint or basil before blending can give a sweet herbal lift to your cocktail. Here are some flavor combinations we recommend:

- Watermelon and cucumber
- Honeydew and nectarine
- Peach and blueberry
- Guava and passion fruit
- Clementine orange and apricot
- Persimmon and red grapes
- Cantaloupe and mint
- Strawberry and basil

FRESH FACTOR
A BLENDER-FRIENDLY JUICE
The fruits in this juice aren't optimal for a typical citrus juicer, but they're perfect for a quick run through the blender. It's a sweet addition to a Life of the Party cocktail.

Grape-Strawberry Juice

▸ 8 ounces of green grapes
▸ 4 ounces of strawberries

Puree fruits in the blender until smooth—about one minute. Pour through fine strainer, pressing down on solids to push out juice. This yields about eight ounces of juice.

Homemade Flavored Syrups

In Chapter 5, "Homemade Flavored Syrup and Soda," you learned the easiest way to turn fresh ingredients into something you can use in the sweet part of your cocktail ratio. You don't have to worry about how "juice-able" a fruit is since you are just chopping it up and throwing it in a pot. You also can relax about any tartness or lack of sweetness in the fruit, since you are adding sugar. And while you don't want to ever use spoiled or moldy fruit, making syrup is a great way to use up fruit that is starting to go a little soft.

DIY *Gourmet*
cranberry-pear syrup

Making flavored syrup gives you a lot of freedom about what goes in your drink. Even a tart ingredient like cranberry will work as a sweet in syrup form.

Cranberry-Pear Syrup

▸ 1 cup water
▸ 1 cup sugar
▸ Half a pear
▸ ¼ cup cranberries

Follow the instructions for Flavored Syrup in Chapter 5, "Homemade Flavored Syrup and Soda."

Here are some flavor combinations that work well as syrups for Life of the Party cocktails:

- Nectarine and plum
- Pineapple and mango
- Blueberry and strawberry
- Apple and raspberry

Homemade Liqueur Substitute

Liqueurs are basically sweetened and flavored liquor, so this is an easy way to get creative with flavor combinations You can concoct your own liqueur substitute by making a flavored syrup, chopping up some fruit, and letting it all steep in some liquor for a few days.

Why don't we tell you exactly how many days to steep your fruit? Different ingredients have different flavor intensities. So, just like you discovered when we made infused spirits in Chapter 3, "Home-Infused Spirits," you'll find that the fruits we use to make liqueur substitutes will have different steeping times, too.

Intense flavors like herbs, spice, and citrus will only need one to two days. Milder flavors like melons, berries, stone fruits, and tropical fruits will need three to four days. Generally, five days should be enough time to let the flavor loose even for subtle flavors like banana.

Vodka is relatively inexpensive and mixes well with all fruit flavors, so it's the simple choice for the job. However, you can take a cue from commercially produced liqueurs and use rum, Cognac, or another spirit as the base for your homemade liqueur substitute.

You'll have to adjust the steeping time based on the ingredients you choose, so taste it periodically until it's just right.

Like homemade syrups, this liqueur concoction gives you free rein on which flavors to include. And, since it's not as sweet as a syrup, it's a flexible mixing ingredient. Here are some flavor combinations that we love in a homemade liqueur:

- Blackberries, blueberries, and Cognac
- Peaches, strawberries, and vodka
- Cherries and brandy
- Bananas, apples, and rum
- Apricot, raspberry, and rum
- Black currants and vodka

Homemade Liqueur Substitute

▸ 3 parts chopped fruit
▸ 1 part water
▸ 1 part sugar
▸ 1½ parts spirit

Place one part of the fruit in a glass jar. Set aside. In a saucepan, combine water, sugar, and the remaining two parts of the fruit. Bring to a boil and simmer for about three minutes. Let cool. Then strain out and discard the solids and refrigerate the syrup for at least ten minutes. Place the refrigerated syrup and the spirit in the jar with the fruit. Seal the jar and shake the mixture. Steep for one to five days, shaking once a day. Strain out the fruit through an ultrafine mesh strainer. Store in a bottle as you would any other liqueur. Refrigeration isn't necessary.

If you're really in a pinch, the following recipe for a flavored-syrup-and-vodka mix is a quick stand-in for a liqueur.

Last-Minute Liqueur Substitute

▸ 2 parts water
▸ 2 parts sugar
▸ 2 parts chopped fruit
▸ 3 parts vodka

Boil the water, sugar, and fruit for about three minutes in a covered saucepan. Let it cool, strain out the solids, and refrigerate the liquid. Combine the vodka and the cooled fruit mixture. If you use a one quarter cup as your unit for parts, this recipe makes about one cup of liqueur substitute, depending on what fruit you use. If you want less or more, adjust it using the ratio. Store in a bottle as you would other liqueur. Refrigeration isn't necessary.

Here's a drink we designed using a last-minute liqueur substitute.

Peachy Keen

INGREDIENTS	RATIO
3 parts bourbon	3 parts strong
2 parts peach-honey liqueur*	2 parts sweet
1 part lemon juice	1 part sour

Pour all ingredients into a cocktail shaker with ice and shake for about fifteen seconds. Strain into a chilled cocktail glass. *Optional:* Freeze two peach slices and place them in the glass.

*Honey-Peach Last-Minute Liqueur

▸ 2 parts water
▸ 2 parts honey
▸ 2 parts peeled and chopped peaches
▸ 3 parts vodka

Follow instructions for the Last-Minute Liqueur Substitute.

DIY *Gourmet*
pineapple-kiwi liqueur substitute

Fruit liqueurs are an essential part of adding flavor to Life of the Party cocktails. Here's one substitute made with an exotic fruit combination you're not likely to find in stores.

Pineapple-Kiwi Liqueur Substitute

- ▶ I part water
- ▶ I part sugar
- ▶ 3 parts chopped pineapple and kiwi
- ▶ I ½ parts vodka

Follow the instructions for the Homemade Liqueur Substitute. This mixture should steep for three to four days, and be strained through an ultra-fine mesh strainer.

Ditch the Recipe— Use the Ratio

Now you're armed with the ability to customize the sweet, strong, and sour parts of the Life of the Party ratio. Before you try it on your own, we'll show you how we used these principles to create our own special cocktail. We dreamed this cocktail up so we could cool down on a hot summer day. At first glance, it looks pretty complicated, but once we explain how we got from basket of ingredients to fabulous cocktail, you'll see how creating a drink like this isn't the province of professionals. It's something you can do in your own kitchen, with your favorite ingredients.

Watermelon-Cucumber Refresher

INGREDIENTS	RATIO	TOTAL
3 parts vodka	3 parts strong	3 parts strong
I part triple sec	I part sweet	2 parts sweet
I part watermelon-cucumber-mint juice*	I part sweet	
I part lime juice	I part sour	I part sour

Pour all ingredients into a cocktail shaker with ice and shake for about fifteen seconds. Strain into a chilled cocktail glass. *Optional:* Freeze two watermelon chunks and place them inside the glass. Garnish with a cucumber slice and a sprig of mint.

Watermelon-Cucumber Refresher

*Watermelon-Cucumber-Mint Juice

▸ 2 parts chopped watermelon

▸ 1 part peeled and chopped cucumber

▸ 2 sprigs of mint

Blend all ingredients together and strain through fine-mesh strainer.

How Did We Do That?

We started out knowing that we wanted to use watermelon, which is moderately sweet and rounds out flavors. But watermelon wasn't enough for us; we wanted more! So the next step was to ask ourselves, "What other ingredient is similar to watermelon in taste but is also a little less sweet so the watermelon can be the dominant sweet flavor?" Turns out a cucumber is a lot like a milder, slightly more tart melon: It's not going to overpower, but it will offer a little hint of tartness to add another layer to our concoction. With all these fresh, juicy ingredients, we wanted a little bit of oomph—something to give it that fresh-from-the-garden taste. Mint is a sweet herb that has a cooling effect, just what we want on a hot day. However, these ingredients are light and mild—liquor and lime juice could easily overpower them. To add enough sweetness to round out the acidity of the lime, we knew we'd need something sweeter with a little weight to it. We always have triple sec in the liquor cabinet, and its orange flavor is a nice complement to lime.

That's a lot of ingredients to fit into one little ratio. But when you look carefully you'll recognize the same flavor categories and ratio that make a Margarita taste good:

3 PARTS STRONG That's vodka. We chose vodka because it is a friendly spirit—you won't find a flavor it doesn't mix well with—and we wanted to introduce a lot of other flavors to the party.

2 PARTS SWEET Remember how a Cosmo uses two different ingredients for its sweet—a juice and a liqueur? That's basically what we did here. Only instead of using just one juice flavor we chose three—cucumber, mint, and watermelon—and combined them in the blender. Here's where you'll use fresh fruits and herbs of your choice.

I PART SOUR You'll recognize good old lime juice, one of the basic sours. Since we had so much going on in the sweet, the simplest way to balance the cocktail was to use limes for acidity.

Your Turn

You've seen what we did with this ratio. Now it's your turn to design a delicious cocktail. To start, just ask yourself the same questions we asked ourselves when creating the Watermelon-Cucumber Refresher:

- What flavor do I want to be the star of the show?
- What other flavor is similar to this one, only milder?
- What other flavor will enhance what I like about these two ingredients?

- What is the best method to make these ingredients cocktail-ready?
- Will this have a pleasing texture?
- What will contrast this flavor without overpowering it?
- What spirit will complement or allow these flavors to shine?

Consult the Flavor Profile Chart in the Appendix to find out the friends and foes of each ingredient as you design your drink. The most important part of picking your ingredients is to taste each one separately to understand how it will work. This step helps you make the cocktail in your mind before you put it in the shaker. Then, once you know what the ingredients taste like alone, you're ready to mix!

Adjusting Your Life of the Party Cocktail

After you mix the drink, take a little taste to see if any adjustments are needed. Remember: If you're making the drink for someone else, you can just dip a straw into the glass and place your finger over the top of the straw to grab some without drinking out of someone else's glass. Even the pros don't get it perfect on the first try every time. But by following the ratio, you'll find that adjustments are minimal—an extra splash of this or twist of that.

TOO STRONG? Add sweet to taste. If you add sour instead of sweet, you're just going to have to add more sweet to make up for it, and you could end up adding things all night.

TOO SWEET? Add sour to taste. You should only add more liquor if you want to taste more liquor; it's never a good way to adjust sweet or sour flavors in an already mixed drink. Plus, it's your most expensive ingredient.

TOO SOUR? Add sweet to taste—carefully and slowly. It's easy to underestimate how sour just a little more citrus juice will make your cocktail.

TOO BITTER? It is unlikely you'll have this problem using the Life of the Party ratio, since it doesn't call for any bitterness. But in the course of experimentation, a little bitterness can sneak in. A little sweet can fix this. A little bit of sour can actually enhance bitterness, so citrus will not help.

TOO WEAK? Only add more liquor to your cocktail if you cannot taste the liquor as much as you'd like. Add additional spirits slowly and in small quantities.

Notes

Notes

Tropical Drinks

7

Some cocktails feel like a vacation, no matter where you are when you drink them. Tiny umbrellas, pineapple spears, and orchids on your glass transport you to a tropical place. Iconic California tiki bars like Don the Beachcomber in Los Angeles and Trader Vic's in Oakland popped onto the scene in the 1930s, mixing a fun though invented island aesthetic with elaborate cocktails. We're not going to lie: This ratio—four parts strong, three parts sweet, and one part sour—is the most challenging ratio to experiment with, so be prepared for a little more trial and error than usual.

Why It Works

Some Tropical drinks—such as the Piña Colada—are more like smoothies or slushies than cocktails. While they are tasty, the liquor can seem like an afterthought since its flavor is obscured by a panoply of sweet ingredients. The pleasure center in the brain lights up when we taste sweet flavors, so it's no wonder that high-sugar foods and drinks are associated with celebration and leisure. Our ratio for tropical cocktails mixes the best of both worlds. High proportions of strong and sweet play off each other, with just a little bit of sour to balance the drink. Even without a lot of fruit, drinks made with this ratio can evoke the tropics.

This Ratio in Action: The Mai Tai

RATIO 4 parts strong : 3 parts sweet : 1 part sour

Head to Hawaii and you're bound to order a Mai Tai. It's sweet but not cloyingly so. Invented at Trader Vic's (although some folks claim that it was actually a Beachcomber creation), the Mai Tai is one of the most inconsistently mixed cocktails around. Orgeat (pronounced or-zha) is the almond syrup that is part of the drink's trademark flavor. It isn't stocked at many bars, either because of its cost or because businesses are concerned about clients' potential nut allergies. This chapter includes a simple orgeat recipe; you can also find quality bottled versions from Trader Vic's, Trader Tiki, and Fee Brothers, among others.

Mai Tai

INGREDIENTS	RATIO	TOTAL
1½ parts light rum	1½ parts strong	4 parts strong
1½ parts gold rum	1½ parts strong	
1 part dark rum	1 part strong	
2 parts triple sec or orange curaçao	2 parts sweet	3 parts sweet
1 part orgeat (almond syrup)	1 part sweet	
1 part lime juice	1 part sour	1 part sour

Pour all ingredients into a cocktail shaker with ice and shake for about fifteen seconds. Strain into an ice-filled Old Fashioned glass. (Some prefer to float the dark rum on top rather than shaking it in.) *Optional:* Garnish with a speared pineapple chunk, maraschino cherry, and sprig of mint.

Notice that both the strong and sweet parts of the ratio were divided. Many of the drinks in this chapter will pair several kinds of each ingredient for an exciting burst of flavor—just remember to keep count and design carefully!

Customizing the Mai Tai

One could argue that every Mai Tai out there is a variation on the original. Since the drink includes so many ingredients, there's no end to the substitutions you can make. The sweet part of the ratio is the best part to play with; use the rums and lime as an anchor for your exploration. Here are some quick changes that will give you a decidedly different drink.

- Instead of orgeat, use a different flavored syrup with a tropical twist—such as hibiscus grenadine or passion fruit syrup—or an almond liqueur.
- Use another fruit liqueur—like peach, pineapple, or strawberry—as a substitute for triple sec or curaçao.
- Add fruit juice in place of orgeat. Acidic juices like orange or pineapple provide a nice counterpoint.
- Adjust the sweet part of the ratio to reduce one ingredient in favor of another. For example, you could use less orgeat and include liqueur to fill in the blank.

orgeat

If you love tiki drinks, then you probably love an almond syrup known as *orgeat*. It's a key ingredient in the original Mai Tai, although many recipes skip the orgeat or substitute more common syrups, such as grenadine. Orgeat adds a unique, nutty sweetness to a drink that's worth a little extra effort. Making orgeat can be quite involved, but this shortcut recipe captures what's great about orgeat while saving you some time.

Orgeat

▸ 8 ounces sliced almonds
▸ 1 ½ cups sugar
▸ 1 cup water
▸ 3 dashes orange blossom water

Toast almonds at 400 degrees for five minutes, shaking halfway through. Cool almonds and then use a blender or food processor to pulverize them. Heat the sugar and water until it boils. Then add the almonds. Simmer and remove from heat once it starts to boil again. Cover the mixture and let it sit for three to twelve hours. Strain it through cheesecloth, add the orange blossom water, and then shake. Add one tablespoon of vodka to preserve, if desired. The syrup will keep for about a month.

Using a Different Sweet

A popular variation on the Mai Tai is the Pineapple Mai Tai, also known as the Pai Tai. This version is fruitier than the original, and you'll find many people sipping it on the shores of Waikiki.

Pai Tai

INGREDIENTS	RATIO	TOTAL
1½ parts light rum	1½ parts strong	4 parts strong
1½ parts gold rum	1½ parts strong	
1 part dark rum	1 part strong	
1 part Grand Marnier	1 part sweet	3 parts sweet
2 parts pineapple juice	2 parts sweet	
1 part fresh lime juice	1 part sour	1 part sour

Pour all ingredients into a cocktail shaker with ice and shake for about fifteen seconds. Strain into an ice-filled Old Fashioned glass. *Optional:* Garnish with a vanilla orchid and a sprig of mint.

This variation of the Mai Tai, which features orange juice in place of pineapple and brings back a little orgeat, is served at the Royal Hawaiian Hotel in Waikiki.

Waikiki Mai Tai

INGREDIENTS	RATIO	TOTAL
1½ parts light rum	1½ parts strong	4 parts strong
1½ parts gold rum	1½ parts strong	
1 part dark rum	1 part strong	
½ part orgeat	½ part sweet	3 parts sweet
½ part simple syrup	½ part sweet	
2 parts orange juice	2 parts sweet	
1 part fresh lime juice	1 part sour	1 part sour

Pour all ingredients into a cocktail shaker with ice and shake for about fifteen seconds. Strain into an ice-filled Old Fashioned glass. *Optional:* Garnish with a vanilla orchid and a sprig of mint.

The Sweet Spot

Mixing together different forms of sweet gives you the chance to add acidity, spice, and nuttiness to the cocktail. You can easily pick sugary liqueurs and syrups to boost the sweetness if that's your style. Or you could go with more herbal or dry flavors if the sweetness turns you off. With some exploration, you can find a whole host of ways to split up ingredients to add up to three parts sweet.

Your options are:

- Liqueur
- Juice
- Syrup
- Puree
- Cream of coconut
- Any combination of those five

Depending on the sweetness of each ingredient, you can adjust how much of each to use. To keep the right consistency, you're always going to have at least one syrup or liqueur. Too much juice will make the drink thin, since there's a lot of liquor.

Combining a fruit liqueur with a nutty or spiced syrup can help prevent fruity sweetness overload, as can using a spiced or nutty liqueur with a sugar or fruit syrup. If using two fruit flavors, test them together to ensure there's harmony instead of a cacophony of sugar.

Here are some combinations we like:

- Triple sec and orgeat
- Maraschino and orgeat
- Peach liqueur and cinnamon syrup

- Falernum and pineapple syrup
- Coconut liqueur and ginger syrup
- Macadamia nut liqueur and banana syrup
- White crème de cacao and hibiscus grenadine

The Hurricane is a cocktail that uses a variety of sweets. This famous drink's origins are hazy—like a lot of cocktail history—but it was Pat O'Brien's in New Orleans that popularized the drink. Like many Tropical drinks, it's gotten a bad rap thanks to premixed syrups and artificial ingredients. Find a quality passion fruit puree and grenadine, or make your own.

Adding a dash or two of bitters to your Hurricane can temper some of the sweetness. In his version, Dale "King Cocktail" DeGroff uses Galliano, a light, herbal Italian liqueur.

Hurricane

INGREDIENTS	RATIO	TOTAL
2 parts light rum	2 parts strong	4 parts strong
2 parts dark rum	2 parts strong	
I part orange juice	I part sweet	
1½ parts passion fruit puree	1½ parts sweet	3 parts sweet
½ part grenadine	½ part sweet	
I part lime juice	I part sour	I part sour

Pour all ingredients into a cocktail shaker with ice and shake for about fifteen seconds. Strain into an ice-filled Hurricane or Collins glass. *Optional:* Garnish with a slice of orange.

Bahama Mama

INGREDIENTS	RATIO	TOTAL
I part light rum	I part strong	
I part dark rum	I part strong	4 parts strong
I part overproof rum	I part strong	
I part coconut rum	I part strong	
I part coffee liqueur	I part sweet	
2 parts pineapple juice	2 parts sweet	3 parts sweet
I part lemon juice	I part sour	I part sour

Pour all ingredients into a cocktail shaker with ice and shake for about fifteen seconds. Strain into an ice-filled Hurricane or Collins glass. *Optional:* Add a splash of grenadine. Garnish with a pineapple wedge.

Another cocktail that goes hand in hand with lounging on the beach is the Bahama Mama. The long list of ingredients can be a little intimidating to experiment with, but it's a lot of fun once you get going.

The Strong Stuff

Throughout the book, liquor choices are simplified as much as possible. For example, instead of specifying brand names or spirits aged for a certain amount of time, you've seen broad categories most people are familiar with—such as white, gold, or dark rum and silver, reposado, or anejo tequila. Those general groups still work for this chapter. However, Tropical drinks are a fun way to investigate spirits you probably don't see every day, so this section is going to get more specific than usual. Don't be scared.

Rum

Rum is the default choice for the cocktails in this chapter, since it comes from tropical places. Rum is made from molasses. Rhum agricole is rum made from sugar cane. You'll

Hurricane

find that tiki drink enthusiasts are very brand loyal and precise about which kind of rum they use—and for good reason. Unlike spirits such as Cognac or bourbon, there are no regulations about what constitutes rum, so each rum-producing region makes its own style of liquor. The darker the liquor's color, the longer it has been aged and the more refined the flavor. Overproof rum has a higher alcohol content—anywhere from 60 percent to 75 percent, compared with the usual 40 percent.

Here's a quick primer on some of the popular rum-producing regions and their general characteristics:

JAMAICA produces rum ranging from light to rich—so you'll see white, gold, and dark in addition to overproof rums. Full-flavored and aromatic, these rums made with molasses are popular in mixed drinks. Appleton Estate and Myers are two popular Jamaican brands.

PUERTO RICO is another tropical place known for its rum, which is of the molasses variety. It's light-bodied and dry, which makes it a popular choice for mixing, although there are also many richer, aged versions available. Bacardi is the most well-known from the island, but other brands you've seen around include Ron Castillo, Captain Morgan, and Don Q.

BARBADOS makes rums on the lighter, sweeter side of the rum spectrum. These are generally molasses-based. Well-known brands include Mount Gay and Tommy Bahama. You'll see light, gold, dark, and overproof rums.

NICARAGUA produces mostly medium-bodied rums, aged anywhere from four to eighteen years. Flor de Caña is the brand you'll encounter most often, but Plantation Rum is also from this country.

THE VIRGIN ISLANDS produce mostly light, mixing rums made from molasses, though there are a few dark and aged rums from the region. Cruzan, Barton, VooDoo, and Sailor Jerry are a few of the brand names from the area.

MARTINIQUE AND GUADELOUPE, French islands, both produce rhum agricole (made from sugar cane juice) and rum made from molasses (sometimes called rhum industriel). A lot of the aging takes place in used French brandy casks. Neisson Rhum, Rhum JM, and St. James are a few of the brand names of this type.

GUYANA specializes in the sugar cane–based Demerara rhum. Surinam and French Guyana make similar spirits. They're rich and heavy, usually aged for extended periods of time compared with other rums. Overproof, they're best used to blend with lighter rums from other areas. El Dorado, Renegade, and Lemon Hart are Demerara rhums.

Though part of the fun of Tropical drinks involves using several different spirits together, you can still have a good time playing with this ratio using just one spirit. We did this in the Island Nights recipe. We realize that this is a lot of booze for one drink! You can try three parts strong instead of four for a Tropical cocktail with a little less kick. It's fruity, but still lets the spirit shine through.

Island Nights

INGREDIENTS	RATIO	TOTAL
4 parts dark rum	4 parts strong	
1½ parts cinnamon syrup*	1½ parts sweet	3 parts sweet
1½ parts honey liqueur	1½ parts sweet	
1 part lemon juice	1 part sour	1 part sour

Pour all ingredients into a cocktail shaker with ice and shake for about fifteen seconds. Strain into an ice-filled Old Fashioned glass. *Optional:* Garnish with a cinnamon stick.

*Cinnamon Syrup

▸ 1 part sugar
▸ 1 part water
▸ 5 cinnamon sticks, broken in half

Bring all ingredients to a boil. Then simmer for 5 minutes. Remove from heat and let it sit—without removing the cinnamon sticks—for two hours. Strain into a glass container and shake. Store with one cinnamon stick remaining in the mixture.

Tequila and Mezcal

Mexico also produces some spirits that are well-suited to the warm-weather lifestyle. Tequila is best known in the United States, but its less-aged cousin mezcal is gaining in popularity. The two work well together, with mezcal adding a smoky bite to tequila's more aged smoothness. Both are made by distilling juice from the heart of the agave plant.

Tequila

Tequila can only be produced in the Mexican state of Jalisco and a few areas in the states of Guanajuato, Michoacán, Nayarit, and Tamaulipas. There are two types of tequila: mixto (or mixed) and 100 percent blue agave. Tequila mixto must be composed of at least 51 percent Weber blue agave, with the rest distilled from other unspecified sugar sources. Mixtos are sometimes colored and called *joven* or *gold* tequila. This isn't what you want. If you think tequila is hangover bait that tastes like cigarettes and sadness, you may have gotten hammered on a bad mixto in college. What you want is 100 percent blue agave tequila, which comes in four age classifications:

SILVER (also known as blanco or plata), which has been aged for sixty days in any type of barrel

REPOSADO, which has been aged in oak anywhere from sixty days to a year

ANEJO, which has been aged in oak for one to three years

EXTRA ANEJO, which has been aged for more than three years

Less aged tequilas are grassy and hot, with a little pepper bite. The more aged a tequila is, the sweeter and smokier it gets.

The Fuzzy Fiesta uses tequila instead of rum.

If you want a stronger cocktail, increase it to four parts strong per the original ratio.

Fuzzy Fiesta

INGREDIENTS	RATIO	TOTAL
3 parts reposado tequila	3 parts strong	
2 parts peach puree	2 parts sweet	3 parts sweet
1 part triple sec	1 part sweet	
1 part lime juice	1 part sour	1 part sour

Pour all ingredients into a cocktail shaker with ice and shake for about fifteen seconds. Strain into an ice-filled highball glass. *Optional:* Garnish with a lime wedge.

Mezcal

Mezcal is made from another type of agave, the maguey. Most mezcals are made in Oaxaca, a state in southern Mexico, by smoking the agave in a pit with hot rocks covered with agave fronds for days, even weeks. The juice of the roasted agave is then distilled, giving the mezcal its smoky disposition. The locals in Oaxaca mostly drink the smoky mezcal straight, but bartenders are experimenting with it in cocktails. It's sharper and often harsher than tequila, so experiment with care.

Sour Power

The other parts of this ratio are so complicated, it's best to stick to lemon or lime for your sour. Experimenting with grapefruit will lead to some amazing concoctions, but start out with the basics first. There's a lot of sweetness in these cocktails, so lemon and lime are usually necessary.

Living on the Edge . . . of the Glass

Tropical drinks that have several kinds of rum, fruit juice, and syrup often result in a brown mixture that doesn't communicate the colorful nature of what's inside the glass. This is one reason why Tropical and tiki drinks are so elaborately garnished. Tiny umbrellas aside, here are some fun ways you can use garnishes to add island beauty to your cocktail.

- Spear together several fruits and a bit of fresh mint on a toothpick or skewer. Maraschino cherries, strawberries, grapes, slices of guava, or chunks of pineapple, melon, and mango can be combined for dramatic effect.

- Slice some star fruit. You don't need a fancy knife technique to give your cocktail the perfect star-shaped garnish; nature will do the job for you. The aptly named star fruit has a light citrus taste and looks like little stars when sliced.
- Float a lime boat. Cut a lime in half and hollow it out. Put a berry and some mint leaves inside, or maybe a flower. Whatever goes inside shouldn't be too heavy; otherwise the lime boat may sink.

Starfruit

- Hollow out a pineapple by cutting off the top and removing the insides. Garnish becomes glass! Now you have an exotic-looking cup for your cocktail.
- Add an orchid or a hibiscus flower to your drink. These nontoxic island blooms immediately transport you and your drink to the tropics. You can check out the "I Feel Pretty, Oh So Pretty: Garnishing with Flowers" section in Chapter 9 to find out more about using flowers in your cocktails.

Using Homemade Ingredients

These are cocktails you can drink through a straw, after all, so no chunks needed. Skip the muddling for this chapter in favor of smoother, sweeter ways to incorporate fresh fruits. Fruits, nuts, and spices will make their way from your grocery bag to your glass, using some easy techniques you're pretty familiar with at this point.

Fresh Fruit Juice

Tropical juices have made their way to every supermarket—along with a whole lot of added sugar and flavors. Even bottles or cartons that tout themselves as "100 percent juice" usually throw in a lot of grape or apple juice no matter what kind of juice you're actually trying to buy. When you make your own juice, you're in charge of how sweet it is and what the flavor combinations are. Using an electric juicer is the easiest, but as we pointed out in Chapter 6, "Fresh Fruit Juice," with a little extra work you can also do the job with a blender and a strainer.

Horned Melon

Here are some fruits and flavor combinations to create homemade juices that will make you swear you're on vacation:

- Pineapple
- Orange
- Pineapple and papaya
- Grapefruit and papaya
- Orange and mango
- Orange and strawberry
- Mango and kiwi
- Mango and strawberry

As the Flavor Profile Chart in the Appendix shows, many ingredients straddle the line between categories. Pineapples are sweet, but they're more sour than a peach. That tartness or tang is also known as acidity, which is a good way to balance sweetness. The drinks in this chapter aren't meant to be tart, but that doesn't mean we want them to be syrupy. Acidity to the rescue!

Homemade Syrups

By now, you're probably a pro at making flavored syrup. (For a refresher, check Chapter 5, "Homemade Flavored Syrup and Soda") It's the easy way to turn any ingredient into something worthy of the sweet part of your cocktail. Here are some flavors we suggest you boil up for Tropical drinks:

- Mango
- Pineapple and raspberries
- Grapefruit and cinnamon
- Vanilla
- Hibiscus and pomegranate
- Cinnamon
- Kiwi and coconut
- Papaya and orange

Tropical flavors aren't always in the form of fruit. In the Caribbean, spices are also an essential part of the cocktail experience. The spiced recipe that follows uses cinnamon syrup and falernum, a sweet liqueur usually made with cloves, ginger, lime, almonds, and rum.

Cinnamon Sunset

Cinnamon Sunset

INGREDIENTS	RATIO	TOTAL
3½ parts Jamaican rum	3½ parts strong	4 parts strong
½ part overproof rum	½ part strong	
1 part orange juice	1 part sweet	3 parts sweet
1 part cinnamon syrup*	1 part sweet	
1 part falernum	1 part sweet	
1 part lime juice	1 part sour	1 part sour

Pour all ingredients into a cocktail shaker with ice and shake for about fifteen seconds. Strain into an ice-filled highball glass. *Optional:* Garnish with an orange wedge.

*See the recipe for cinnamon syrup with the Island Nights cocktail recipe in this chapter's "Rum" section.

Fresh Cocktail Puree

A cocktail puree falls somewhere between a juice and a syrup. For most purees, all you have to do is peel and chop some fruit, add a little sugar, blend it until smooth, and strain it through a fine sieve. With some fruits, such as kiwi or blueberries, you may not want to add sugar, but overall, one part sugar for every six parts of fruit is enough to eliminate a little tartness, if

desired. You can generally store these in the fridge for a week.

Here are some flavors we suggest for cocktail purees:

- Passion fruit (If you can find it fresh!)
- Guava
- Peach
- Pineapple
- Strawberry
- Raspberry
- Mango
- Nectarine
- Kiwi

You'll see mango nectar in a can, but a homemade mango puree tastes much better in a cocktail. Here's a recipe we developed to show it off.

Hula Man

INGREDIENTS	RATIO	TOTAL
3 parts spiced rum	3 parts strong	4 parts strong
1 part dark rum	1 part strong	
2½ parts mango puree*	2½ parts sweet	3 parts sweet
½ part hibiscus syrup	½ part sweet	
1 part lime juice	1 part sour	1 part sour

Pour all ingredients into a cocktail shaker with ice and shake for about fifteen seconds. Strain into an ice-filled highball glass. *Optional:* Garnish with a hibiscus flower.

*Mango Puree

▸ 1 cup mango, peeled and chopped
▸ ⅓ ounce sugar

Follow instructions given for Fresh Cocktail Puree.

Home-Infused Spirits

With such a high proportion of liquor in your drink, why miss the chance to add some DIY flavor to your spirits? Most tropical fruits release their flavor quickly, so you won't have to wait long!

DIV *Gourmet*
banana rum

Bananas are easy to find and give your cocktail a bright, tropical flavor. You can't juice them, so for a non-blended drink, plan to create a syrup or liqueur. We haven't seen a lot of banana-infused rum around, but we don't know why. It's so tasty, you'll want to drink it straight.

Banana Rum

▸ I part gold rum
▸ I part banana, peeled and sliced

Place the banana slices in a glass jar and cover with gold rum. Let it steep for two to four days, shaking daily. Strain through cheesecloth into your bottle or jar, and store the mixture as you would any other liquor.

Banana rum is one of the infusions you have to be sure to strain carefully. As the banana sits in the rum it releases some goo—yes, that's the technical term—that will go right through a mesh strainer and into your infused liquor if you don't use the cheesecloth. It's a delicious goo to be sure, but it will mess with the texture of your spirit, and it will make your infusion taste like an old, overripe banana in a matter of days.

Here are some infusions we think are perfect for your Tropical cocktail:

- Banana gold rum
- Mango light rum
- Key lime tequila
- Cinnamon vodka
- Pineapple cachaca
- Grapefruit rum
- Ginger vodka
- Peach rum
- Strawberry tequila

The infusions you make for Tropical drinks are flexible enough to use in other cocktails, so feel free to make larger batches of your favorites.

Ditch the Recipe—Use the Ratio

Now that you're done reading about drinking, you're ready to do it. You're an expert on infusing spirits and making syrups, and you even know a thing or two about cocktail purees. We'll show you one of our creations that uses several of these elements before sending you on your way to create your own island masterpieces. We're using the weaker version of the ratio, so those playing along at home can leave it as is or increase to four parts strong.

Volcanic Seduction

INGREDIENTS	RATIO	TOTAL
1½ parts banana-infused rum	1½ parts strong	3 parts strong
1½ parts white rum	1½ parts strong	
½ part triple sec	½ part sweet	3 parts sweet
½ part cream of coconut	½ part sweet	
2 parts strawberry syrup	2 parts sweet	
1 part lime	1 part sour	1 part sour

Pour all ingredients into a cocktail shaker with ice and shake for about fifteen seconds. Strain into an ice-filled Hurricane or Collins glass. *Optional:* Garnish with a strawberry.

How Did We Do That?

Our banana rum was so exciting that we wanted to put it in everything, including coconut cream pie and strawberry shortcake. This cocktail was our way of doing that—because really that's a lot of dessert. We wanted to get those flavors without the sugar overload.

3 PARTS STRONG Since banana rum was our inspiration, the strong part of the ratio was the basis for our fruit matching. It's quite sweet, so we chose to pair it with a light rum, which offers a little heat and tart undertones. Darker rums have a much sweeter character, so we left them out.

3 PARTS SWEET Banana is the main flavor we were trying to accent, so we ran through the list of fruits that were a good match. Strawberry-banana and coconut-banana both sounded amazing, but we couldn't choose. What if we did both? Strawberry, even in syrup form, has a little bit of a tart note compared with the very sweet cream of coconut. So we chose to use more strawberry. We also went with a triple sec to add a little alcohol and thin out the sweet part of our cocktail.

I PART SOUR There is a lot of sweetness in this drink, and lime is best at balancing it since it's louder than lemon.

Your Turn

Tropical cocktails are the most challenging to create because of the long list of ingredients and multiple flavors. But you must love a challenge—otherwise, you'd just be at a bar sipping vodka and orange juice instead of embarking on your own home cocktail adventures. Let's get tropical! Here are the questions to ask as you develop your cocktail:

- What flavor do I want to be the star of the show?
- What form will I use that flavor in? Infusion? Syrup? Puree?
- What other flavor pairs well with my chosen main flavor?
- What other flavor will enhance what I like about these two ingredients?

- What is the best method to make these ingredients cocktail-ready?
- What will contrast with this flavor without overpowering it?
- What spirit will complement or allow these flavors to shine?

Adjusting Your Tropical Cocktail

With so many ingredients, it's easy to end up with a drink that is unbalanced.But if your drink doesn't taste quite right, don't give up! You can tweak your Tropical concoction till it's just right.

TOO STRONG? Try a splash of simple syrup. Chances are you're using multiple sweet ingredients, so adding more of one of those could throw off the balance you've achieved.

TOO SOUR? A little simple syrup can help here, too.

TOO SWEET? A dash or two of bitters can help you out here. If it tastes a little syrupy, a mini-squeeze of citrus might do the job.

TOO BITTER? Although we're not using bitter ingredients, some herbs can add a touch of bitterness. Try a splash of simple syrup. Sour will make it even more bitter, so don't try more citrus.

TOO WEAK? Frankly, this is a rare problem with Tropical drinks. As always, add liquor slowly and carefully if desired.

coconut: water vs. milk vs. cream

There couldn't be a chapter on Tropical drinks that didn't include coconut. But looking at a coconut, it's hard to figure out how this heavy, hairy brown bowling ball can make its way into your glass. Cream of coconut is how! But wait … is that the same as coconut milk? Nope. In fact, cream of coconut isn't even the same thing as coconut cream. Here's the scoop on the different coconut products:

- **COCONUT WATER** Split open a coconut and the juice you'll find inside is the coconut water. You wouldn't use it as a sweet in cocktails. However, it does have a place in the cocktail world—just look at some of the punches in Chapter 11.
- **COCONUT MILK** This is usually made by cooking equal parts coconut and water. You'll see cans of it anywhere you can buy Thai food ingredients, since coconut milk is the basis of Thai curry. It's not typically used for cocktails. Coconut milk has the consistency of dairy milk—there's even a cream that rises to the top.
- **COCONUT CREAM** This is thicker and richer than coconut milk. Coconut cream either consists of the cream that rises to the top of a can of coconut milk or the product that results from cooking four parts coconut with one part water. You could use coconut cream in cocktails, but it isn't as sweet as you'd expect.
- **CREAM OF COCONUT** *This* is the one you use in cocktails! For some reason, whoever names ingredients didn't bother to come up with a very unique name for this stuff. Cream of coconut is coconut cream with sugar added. You'll find this in the cocktail aisle. Brand names include Coco Lopez and Coco Real. ▶

coconut: water vs. milk vs. cream *cont'd*

Cream of coconut has its place in this chapter, but it's most well-known as an ingredient in a blended Piña Colada—a Tropical cocktail that doesn't quite subscribe to the typical Tropical ratio. (Note that if you use vodka instead of rum, you'll have a Chi-Chi.)

Piña Colada

INGREDIENTS	RATIO	TOTAL
1½ parts light rum	1½ parts strong	1½ parts strong
1 part cream of coconut	1 part sweet	3 parts sweet
2 parts pineapple juice	2 parts sweet	
½ part heavy cream	½ part mild	½ part mild
8 parts crushed ice	8 parts weak	8 parts weak

Combine all ingredients in a blender. Once it's smooth, pour into a chilled double Old Fashioned glass or goblet. *Optional:* Add a pineapple chunk when blending for texture. Garnish with a slice of pineapple.

Notes

_____

_____

_____

_____

_____

_____

_____

_____

Notes

RATIO:
1 part strong :
1 part sweet : 2 parts mild

•

FLAGSHIP COCKTAILS:
White Russian, Brandy Alexander,
Grasshopper

Sweet and Creamy

8

iquor is usually the star of the show, with sweet and sour flavors playing supporting roles. In this chapter, liquor shares the spotlight with sweet, while sour gets the night off altogether. The Sweet and Creamy ratio—one part strong, one part sweet, and two parts mild—is at work in drinkable treats like a White Russian and a Brandy Alexander. You can have them any time (well, 9:00 A.M. is probably not a good idea), but these smooth and sweet concoctions make for a great after-dinner delight. Sweet and Creamy cocktails are like dessert: delectable and best enjoyed in moderation.

Why It Works

The Sweet and Creamy ratio is your ticket to mellow cocktails with a hint of richness and warmth. You'll find that each ingredient helps the other out. Previous chapters have shown you how sweet and strong complement each other. The balancing act in Sweet and Creamy cocktails depends on mild ingredients like cream to soften the heat of the base spirit, cut the sugariness of the sweet component, and add texture without adding a competing flavor.

This Ratio in Action: The White Russian

RATIO I part strong : I part sweet : 2 parts mild

Even if you haven't seen the *Big Lebowski*, you're probably familiar with the protagonist's signature drink, a White Russian—or, as The Dude calls it, a Caucasian. Created in the 1960s, it's not the oldest Sweet and Creamy cocktail, but it's arguably the most well-known. It's like latte meets cocktail. Here's our favorite recipe.

White Russian

INGREDIENTS	RATIO
I part vodka	I part strong
I part coffee liqueur	I part sweet
2 parts half-and-half	2 parts mild

Pour all ingredients into a cocktail shaker with ice and shake for about thirty seconds. Strain into a chilled cocktail glass.

We favor this recipe over other variations because too much vodka and not enough half-and-half ends up giving the drink a watery texture with most of the emphasis on the coffee liqueur—which can be a little like pouring vodka in a weak cup of overly sugared coffee.

Customizing the White Russian

Do some simple substitutions, and you can turn a White Russian into any number of new cocktails. What makes coffee liqueurs like Kahlua, Tia Maria, and Copa de Oro work well in Sweet and Creamy cocktails is the way the liqueur's sweetness is balanced with a touch of bitterness. Look for flavors with characteristics that remind you of coffee, and you'll come up with a whole list of liqueurs made with nuts, roots, and spices that add complexity and depth to the sweet element of your cocktail. Some you can try are:

- Hazelnut
- Black tea
- Root beer
- Pistachio
- Gingerbread
- Macadamia nut
- Chocolate
- Crème de cacao

The coffee bean and the cacao bean have a lot in common, so it's not a stretch to assume that replacing the coffee liqueur in a White Russian with chocolate liqueur would make for a great cocktail. In fact, we know it does: It gives you a Chocolate Cream Martini.

Chocolate Cream Martini

INGREDIENTS	RATIO
I part vodka	I part strong
I part chocolate liqueur	I part sweet
2 parts half-and-half or light cream	2 parts mild

Pour all ingredients into a cocktail shaker with ice and shake for about thirty seconds. Strain into a chilled cocktail glass.

Chocolate Cream Martini

DIY *Gourmet*
chocolate liqueur

One way to feed your Chocolate Martini addiction is to make your own chocolate liqueur. It's delicious in a variety of cocktails, and it's easy to make. Here's how.

Chocolate Liqueur

▸ I liter rum or vodka
▸ 2 vanilla beans, split lengthwise
▸ ½ cup cocoa nibs

Follow instructions for Homemade Liqueur Substitute in Chapter 6, "Homemade Liqueur Substitute." This mixture should steep for three weeks.

Using a Different Spirit

Before looking at fancier ways you can customize this ratio—such as making your own liqueur and syrups and using fresh fruit—here's what happens when you do another simple substitution, this time in the strong part of the ratio.

For more than eighty-five years, the Alexander has been pleasing palates.

The version made with brandy is the most famous—TV characters from Mary Richards on the *Mary Tyler Moore Show* to Peggy Olson on *Mad Men* have ordered one, and Feist even named a song after it. Let's take a look at how you can turn that chocolate and cream combo into an old-fashioned pleasure.

Brandy Alexander

INGREDIENTS	RATIO
I part brandy	I part liquor
I part dark crème de cacao	I part sweet
2 parts heavy cream	2 parts mild

Pour all ingredients into a cocktail shaker with ice and shake for about thirty seconds. Strain into a chilled cocktail glass.

During Prohibition, the Alexander was made with genever-style gin, which was often made in a bathtub. Genever is making a comeback—minus the bathtub—and like most spirits aged in oak, it does well in a Sweet and Creamy cocktail. The honeyed undertones of rum, brandy, and whiskey make them well-suited to these dessert creations. Brandy tastes great in a sweet and creamy cocktail, so try this whiskey-based drink.

Irish Thanksgiving

INGREDIENTS	RATIO
1 part Irish whiskey	1 part liquor
1 part pumpkin spice liqueur	1 part sweet
2 parts half-and-half	2 parts mild

Pour all ingredients into a cocktail shaker with ice and shake for about thirty seconds. Strain into a chilled cocktail glass.

The Sweet Spot

Just like Life of the Party cocktails, the potential for inventiveness in Sweet and Creamy drinks lies in the sweet part of the ratio. By using more than one liqueur or using ingredients other than liqueur to sweeten your cocktail, you add even more cocktails to your repertoire.

There are four ways to add sweetness to your Sweet and Creamy cocktail:

1. 1 part liqueur
2. 2 parts liqueur (replacing liquor with liqueur)
3. ½ part liqueur + ½ part liqueur (using two different liqueurs)
4. 1 part fruit muddled in syrup or liqueur

Liqueurs

You've already done simple substitutions with liqueur—using one liqueur instead of another for the sweet portion of the Sweet and Creamy ratio. Some other liqueurs that taste great in this type of cocktail are:

- Banana liqueur
- Crème de banane
- Mango liqueur
- Crème de menthe
- White chocolate liqueur
- Strawberry liqueur
- Pecan liqueur

Floral and herbal liqueurs, such as elderberry liqueur or Chartreuse, are more difficult to balance in a Sweet and Creamy drink. If you do try those, you'll also need a very sweet liqueur to smooth the flavors—and it won't always work. For this reason, we don't recommend floral and herbal liqueurs for Sweet and Creamy cocktails.

Since using liqueur is the simplest way to add flavor to your Sweet and Creamy cocktail, using two liqueurs is the simplest way to add two flavors.

Banana and honey are natural companions, and they're an easy-to-imagine combination for this split. Honey has an intense flavor, while banana's sweetness is mellow with a slight hint of tartness. This complementary relationship inspired the following recipe for a Sweet and Creamy cocktail using two liqueurs:

Banana Cream Buzz

INGREDIENTS	RATIO	TOTAL
I part Cognac	I part strong	I part strong
½ part crème de banane	½ part sweet	I part sweet
½ part honey liqueur	½ part sweet	
2 parts half-and-half	2 parts mild	2 parts mild

Pour all ingredients into a cocktail shaker with ice and shake for about thirty seconds. Strain into a chilled cocktail glass. *Optional:* Add two to three dashes of orange bitters.

Some other combinations that work well in a Sweet and Creamy cocktail are:

- Crème de menthe and chocolate liqueur
- Pineapple liqueur and mango liqueur
- Coffee liqueur and crème de cacao
- Hazelnut liqueur and chocolate liqueur
- Coffee liqueur and hazelnut liqueur
- Strawberry liqueur and banana liqueur
- Almond liqueur and cherry liqueur

Grab your favorite liqueurs (or maybe some you've never tried) and experiment with new flavor combinations. Pick two and mix them together in equal parts. Little sample bottles are perfect for this purpose.

Doubling the Liqueur

There are actually several well-known Sweet and Creamy cocktails that don't use spirits at all. If you want a drinkable dessert, you can leave out the liquor and instead double the amount of liqueur you use.

In addition to the liqueur combinations found earlier in this chapter, here are some others you could use if you skipped the spirits:

- White crème de cacao and crème de banane
- Raspberry liqueur and limoncello crème
- Hazelnut liqueur and dark crème de cacao
- Almond liqueur and pumpkin spice liqueur
- Pomegranate liqueur and white chocolate liqueur

Here's a cocktail you've heard of that doubles the liqueur in the ratio:

Grasshopper

INGREDIENTS	RATIO
1 part green crème de menthe	1 part sweet (replacing 1 part strong)
1 part white crème de cacao	1 part sweet
2 parts heavy cream	2 parts mild

Pour all ingredients into a cocktail shaker with ice and shake for about thirty seconds. Strain into a chilled cocktail glass.

MIXOLOGY 101
cream vs. crème

Sometimes it seems to take a special dictionary to navigate the cocktail world. For instance, while it's true that *crème* is the French word for *cream*, a crème liqueur and a cream liqueur are not the same. Cream liqueurs, such as Bailey's or Carolans Irish cream, contain dairy cream. Crème liqueurs, such as crème de menthe and crème de cacao, have more sugar than other liqueurs and therefore a thicker consistency. They don't actually contain any cream. Crème and cream liqueurs are both sweeter and heavier than other liqueurs. So remember that crème de cacao, chocolate cream liqueur, and chocolate liqueur are three different things. Taste your liqueur separately before mixing with abandon.

Switch it up a little, and you end up with a Coffee Grasshopper.

Coffee Grasshopper

INGREDIENTS	RATIO
1 part green crème de menthe	1 part sweet (replacing 1 part strong)
1 part coffee liqueur	1 part sweet
2 parts heavy cream	2 parts mild

Pour all ingredients into a cocktail shaker with ice and shake for about thirty seconds. Strain into a chilled cocktail glass.

The Strong Stuff

So far you've seen Sweet and Creamy cocktails made with vodka, brandy, and Irish whiskey. Some spirits work better than others. In general, neutral spirits or oaky spirits are the easiest to mix in this type of cocktail. Be sure to taste each ingredient separately to see if you think they'll taste good together. To make that job a little easier, here are our spirits recommendations for Sweet and Creamy cocktails. Keep in mind that the brand does make a difference—these are simply general characteristics.

Vodka

Vodka is an adventurous mixologist's safety spirit. It has very little flavor of its own, so it contributes dryness to your drink without taking over.

Genever-Style Gin

Think of whiskey without the wood complexity or honey flavors that come from aging, and you'll have an idea what this spirit is like. It imparts some mild citrus flavor, so it's not as neutral as vodka—but it's another great one for adding warmth without adding too many layers of flavor.

Dark Rum

This liquor is much smoother and less astringent than its lighter counterpart, white rum. It can be slightly nutty or have undertones of coffee or molasses. Generally, it's rich with some sweetness tempered by a bit of bitterness.

Brandy

Made from grapes, this category of spirit includes Cognac and Armagnac. Hints of oak and sweetness make it a wonderful companion to rich flavors.

Bourbon

Bourbon is a type of whiskey made primarily from corn. It's a little sweeter than brandy but shares its basic characteristics. You might find notes of vanilla, brown sugar, or honey to play with.

Scotch

This can be a tricky one to use, since scotch varies dramatically based on the region and style. Skip the smoky and peaty Islay or Highland scotches in favor of mild and sweeter Speyside or Lowland scotches or a mild blend.

Irish Whiskey

This style of spirit is a little thinner and less sweet than other types of whiskey. It makes for a good mixer when you're looking for a little heat and light smoke that doesn't interfere with your mixers.

GAG REEL

TEQUILA, DRY GIN, AND "OVERPROOF" SPIRITS VS. CREAM

If you're really determined to mix tequila, dry gin, or very high-proof spirits with cream, you can probably find a delicious way if you work hard at it. There are great drinks out there that do just that. But when it comes to home mixing, your chance of failure far outweighs your chance of success if you use those spirits.

Tequila has strong pepper, mineral, and grassy flavors that seem to get even stronger instead of mellowing when combined with cream. This makes the sweet element almost invisible and can end up tasting a little like a thick, burnt match.

Dry gin—not to be confused with the highly mixable genever-style gin—is more cream-friendly than tequila, but it tends to clash with many of the liqueurs that shine in Sweet and Creamy cocktails. Just imagine chocolate or coffee battling a pine tree.

High-proof liquors like Everclear, sometimes called *overproof spirits,* are too hot and overpowering to blend well in a cool and smooth dessert cocktail.

Infused Spirits

A simple way to tweak the strong part of your Sweet and Creamy cocktail is to use a flavor-infused spirit. For years, these flavor infusions were cloyingly sweet or artificial tasting. While a few still suffer this character flaw, most liquor makers are now appealing to a more sophisticated cocktail enthusiast interested in complex, natural flavors. You can always use your own home-infused spirits and homemade liqueur substitutes.

Speaking of flavored liquors, tea has made its way into all the cocktail hot spots. Here's a creation we made with sweet tea vodka.

Tea Time

Tea Time

INGREDIENTS	RATIO
1 part sweet tea vodka	1 part strong
1 part white crème de menthe	1 part sweet
2 parts half-and-half	2 parts mild

Pour all ingredients into a cocktail shaker with ice and shake for about thirty seconds. Strain into a chilled cocktail glass.

Mild Child

For the mild part of the ratio, milk- and cream-based ingredients work best. The amount of fat in your mild mixer dictates how thick and versatile it is. For instance, milk has less fat than cream. However, because milk is much thinner than cream, it will not do as much to change the texture of your cocktail when shaken. Also, it will not do as much to balance strong flavors. Non-dairy substitutes such as soy or rice milk are even thinner than dairy milk; they generally won't perform well in this type of cocktail for the same reason.

Here's the skinny on the "creamy" part of Sweet and Creamy cocktails. We averaged these fat percentages using U.S. standards, so check your cartons for exact numbers.

Milk

Since it's usually labeled by fat content, the percentage of fat isn't hard to figure out for milk. Whole milk is 3.25 percent, and it goes down in increments all the way to .5 percent from there. While you can use milk for the cocktails in this chapter, they will be thinner and less complex. Tweaking the ratio can help with that, but they won't be perfect.

Half-and-half

As the name suggests, this is half milk and half cream—resulting in 12 percent fat. It's our choice for most creamy cocktails because it adds body and blends well but isn't too heavy. It isn't possible to make true half-and-half without fat, since the inclusion of cream means the inclusion of fat. Milk products sold as fat-free half-and-half contain sugar or corn syrup along with other thickening ingredients and simply do not behave the same as regular half-and-half in a cocktail.

Light Cream and Light Whipping Cream

At 20 percent fat, light cream is a good substitute for heavy cream when half-and-half just doesn't add enough smoothness. Light whipping cream, which is 30 percent fat, is another compromise cream to try before getting to the big guns. Overall, either of these will perform well, since we're not actually whipping them to make a standing cream.

Heavy Cream and Heavy Whipping Cream

It's no wonder these taste so good: Both varieties have 38 percent fat. Though it may sound counterintuitive, heavy cream does the best job of balancing out heavier ingredients like cream liqueurs and crème liqueurs.

Using Homemade Ingredients

The ingredients in these cocktails should have a syrupy or rich texture so they can blend well and cling together. That's why we'll be combining muddled fruit with syrup or liqueur to thicken it up. You may even want to throw in a sweet herb, such as basil or mint. Before you play with fresh ingredients, here are the techniques you'll be using.

Muddling Fresh Fruit with Liqueur

In Chapter 2, you learned how to muddle—which is just a fancy cocktail term for smash. To ensure sweetness and a thick mouthfeel, you can muddle your fruit in liqueur before shaking it with the other cocktail ingredients. Some liqueur combinations that we like in Sweet and Creamy cocktails are:

- Chocolate liqueur and strawberries
- Banana liqueur and pineapples
- Crème de menthe and peaches
- Raspberry liqueur and apricots
- Hazelnut liqueur and cherries
- Crème de cacao and mint and blackberries

Because the ratio already calls for a form of cream, we didn't include any cream liqueurs on our list of recommended liqueur substitutions. However, cream liqueurs can work really well when muddled with fruit. Try combining the homemade liqueur substitutions you learned to make in Chapter 6, "Homemade Liqueur Substitute" with fruit to complement the flavor!

Muddling Fresh Fruit in Syrup

Syrup is another way to thicken up your fruit while muddling. Also, as you learned in Chapter 5, "Homemade Flavored Syrup and Soda," you can make your own syrups using fresh fruit and herbs—use a variety of fresh ingredients you prepare yourself. Whether you buy a syrup or make your own, here are some syrup and fruit combinations that taste great in a Sweet and Creamy cocktail:

- Tangerine-lavender syrup and nectarines
- Lychee syrup and mangoes
- Orange syrup and persimmon
- Vanilla syrup and raspberries

On the Edge . . . of the Glass

These sweet treats cry out for creative rims—an extra touch of flavoring on the edge of your glass. Moisten the edge of the glass with simple syrup and then roll it in the ingredient that best complements your cocktail. Try:

- Unsweetened cocoa powder
- Ground cocoa nibs
- Crushed gingerbread cookies
- Crushed vanilla wafers
- Grated coconut
- Grated white chocolate

ice ice, baby

Why are these cocktails shaken instead of served over ice? Some White Russian recipes say to build the drink—pour ingredients in one at a time in a glass full of ice—and stir. This might be pretty to look at . . . but not for long. Unless you gulp it down, a stirred White Russian starts to look pretty unappealing as the cream changes consistency and the ice melts. Shaking a drink with cream in it ensures that the ingredients will actually mix. This not only looks better, but it tastes more blended too.

Ditch the Recipe— Use the Ratio

At this point, you know how to make substitutions to customize a well-known Sweet and Creamy cocktail recipe. You know you can incorporate fresh ingredients with muddling, but you haven't actually done it yet. Now it's time to start getting creative. With a little brainpower and testing, you can construct your own mixed masterpiece. We designed the following two Sweet and Creamy cocktails using muddled fruit to show you how.

Strawberries dipped in white chocolate are irresistible; the same is true for that flavor combination in cocktail form. Here's a recipe that mixes fruit and cream liqueur for the sweet part of the ratio.

Pink Frost

INGREDIENTS	RATIO
I part dark rum	I part strong
I part strawberries muddled in white chocolate cream liqueur	I part sweet
2 parts half-and-half	2 parts mild

Pour all ingredients into a cocktail shaker with ice and shake for about thirty seconds. Strain into a chilled cocktail glass. *Optional:* Garnish with shaved white chocolate and a strawberry slice.

But what if you want to use a sweet herb? Now that you've seen an example using fruit and liqueur, check out a refreshing cocktail that uses an herb and syrup for the sweet part of the Sweet and Creamy ratio to create a creamy Mint Julep kind of experience.

Kentucky Peach

INGREDIENTS	RATIO
1 part bourbon	1 part strong
1 part mint muddled in peach syrup*	1 part sweet
2 parts light cream	2 parts mild

Pour all ingredients into a cocktail shaker with ice and shake for about thirty seconds. Strain into a chilled cocktail glass.

*Peach Syrup

▸ 1 part sugar

▸ 1 part water

▸ 1 part fresh peaches, peeled and chopped

Follow the instructions for Flavored Syrup in Chapter 5, "Homemade Flavored Syrup and Soda."

How Did We Do That?

You're a long way from White Russians now! Or are you? Take a look at how we created the Pink Frost and the Kentucky Peach, because you'll recognize the same concepts at work.

Pink Frost

1 PART STRONG That's the dark rum. We wanted something with a medium-sweet character and a little heat to balance the two sweet ingredients we planned to incorporate.

1 PART SWEET White chocolate and strawberry flavors sounded delicious, and we wanted to use fresh fruit. We split one part sweet by using strawberries and white chocolate cream liqueur, muddling them together to marry the flavors. Strawberries and white chocolate is a very sweet combination—adding anything more would make the drink taste muddy and unrefined.

2 PARTS MILD Half-and-half is your go-to mild, and it gets the job done perfectly here. If you want your cocktail to stiffen like whipped cream you could go for a higher-fat mild like heavy cream.

Kentucky Peach

I PART STRONG Bourbon has a lot of character, so we wanted it to be the strongest flavor in the cocktail. The oak and honey notes are what we're building this cocktail around.

I PART SWEET Mint is a great comple-ment to bourbon—just think of this drink's inspiration, the Mint Julep. The subtle pairing benefits from a more traditionally sweet fruit ingredi-ent like peach. Also, peaches comple-ment bourbon as well as mint, so we chose those two flavors for our sweet. Muddling is the most effective way to add mint flavor to a cocktail. To add some thickness and sweetness, we knew we'd need a syrup or liqueur. We found peach liqueurs too intense for this, so we made our own peach syrup. Dividing the sweet, we used fresh mint and peach syrup. A little muddling married the two flavors together.

2 PARTS MILD We went with a light cream rather than half-and-half to add a little weight and stiffness to the cocktail.

Your Turn

We've been hogging all the fun. So now it's your turn to design your own Sweet and Creamy cocktail. When choosing your ingredients, just ask yourself the same questions we asked ourselves as we created the Pink Frost and the Kentucky Peach:

- What flavor do I want to be the star of the show?
- What other flavor complements my chosen star flavor?
- Will another flavor enhance what I like about these two ingredients together, or will it cause chaos?
- What is the best method to make these ingredients cocktail-ready?
- How will cream interact with my chosen ingredients?
- If the base spirit is not part of the main flavor combination, which spirit will most complement my chosen flavor combination or recede into the background to let it shine?

For inspiration, check the Flavor Profile Chart in the Appendix.

Adjusting Your Sweet and Creamy Cocktail

Ingredients vary, so some of your drinks will require a little tweak to get them just right. Remember to shake the mixture again after adding additional ingredients. Take a little sip. If it's not perfect, use this adjustment strategy:

TOO STRONG? This is not likely to happen with Sweet and Creamy cocktails unless you use a particularly strong spirit. Add a little bit of your sweet to taste and shake the drink again. Resist the urge to add more mild.

TOO SWEET? Add more spirits if you feel it is lacking that liquor bite and depth. But don't simply pour in booze to cut the sweetness: Examine the sweet part of your ratio. If you used fruit muddled in syrup or liqueur, maybe you need to add more—which often adds a bit of tartness to balance the sweet. If you used two liqueurs, perhaps some fresh fruit can save the day—for instance fresh raspberries will balance the sweetness of raspberry liqueur. In general, it's best to avoid citrus for this ratio, but a couple dashes of orange bitters can tempter sweetness. Don't go too crazy—if you can taste the bitters, you've gone too far.

TOO CREAMY? Make sure you had enough thickness in the sweet part of your ratio. If not, bulk it up with a little syrup. You may have depended too much on fresh fruit or herbs, in which case a little liqueur can help. Adding liquor will change the flavor dramatically, so don't use this to dilute your drink.

TOO WEAK? If you cannot taste the liquor as much as you'd like to, add additional spirits slowly and in small quantities.

Notes

Notes

RATIO:
2 parts strong :
1 part sweet : 1 part sour

•

FLAGSHIP COCKTAILS:
Daiquiri, Aviation, Jack Rose,
Bee's Knees

Elegant Sips

9

I magine yourself sipping cocktails in the 1930s. Are you at a London club with Hollywood stars escaping Prohibition, or are you high above the earth in an airplane that's more like a flying cocktail lounge than the sardine-can air transportation we experience today? Maybe you're an expatriate working on your art in Havana or Paris. This ratio will help you create evocative drinks that will make you feel like you're there. You're going to have fun with floral, herbal, and spiced ingredients in the sweet part of the ratio in this chapter. The Elegant Sips ratio—two parts strong, one part sweet, and one part sour—is a way of capturing the glamour of cocktails past. Like the Life of the Party drinks in Chapter 6, the drinks in this chapter are part of a family of cocktails that bartenders call "Sours." However, the Life of the Party creations are usually quite sweet, while the Elegant Sips cocktails have a much tarter character.

Why It Works

The sweet and sour ingredients in Elegant Sips cocktails will enhance the spirits you use rather than obscure them. Think of this ratio's balancing act as a seesaw—with spirits on one side and a combination of sweet and sour on the other. Before the drink even hits your taste buds, the herbs, flowers, or spices in the cocktail reach your nose and conjure a delicate sweetness without additional sugar. The scent and flavor of fresh citrus creates an invigorating cocktail that awakens your senses.

This Ratio in Action: The Daiquiri

RATIO 2 parts strong : 1 part sweet : 1 part sour

A simple cocktail, the classic Daiquiri barely resembles the slushy, fruity drinks you're accustomed to seeing under that name on restaurant menus. It's just white rum, sugar, and lime shaken with ice. The Mojito in Chapter 10 has a lot in common with the Daiquiri. Both are Cuban creations, and as you'll see, they love them some lime. If you do, too, then you'll love this basic Daiquiri recipe.

Daiquiri

INGREDIENTS	RATIO
2 parts white rum	2 parts strong
1 part simple syrup	1 part sweet
1 part lime juice	1 part sour

Pour ingredients into a cocktail shaker with ice and shake for about fifteen seconds. Strain into a chilled cocktail glass.

Customizing the Daiquiri

The minimalist Daiquiri is easy and fun to personalize. Its three ingredients each open themselves up to a little fooling around. Here are some quick ways to make the Daiquiri your own:

USE AN INFUSED SPIRIT. Strawberries, mango, orange, ginger, mint, you name it—almost any flavor goes well with white rum and lime.

TRY A FLAVORED SYRUP. Simple syrup makes a simple Daiquiri. Buy or make your own flavored syrup with fruit or herbs to add another level to your cocktail. Basil, papaya, green tea, kiwi, guava, raspberries . . . get creative.

SUBSTITUTE ANOTHER CITRUS. Replace or augment the lime juice with lemon, grapefruit, tangerine, or orange to switch up your Daiquiri.

Adding Another Sweet and Sour

To many, Ernest Hemingway is as well-known for the Daiquiri variation that bears his name as he is for his writing. Part of the simple syrup in the original is replaced with maraschino liqueur, and grapefruit juice takes the place of some of the lime juice. Legend has it that at the iconic Havana bar Floridita, he downed sixteen of them in one night. We wouldn't have been able to read a book let alone write one if we did that.

Hemingway Daiquiri

INGREDIENTS	RATIO	TOTAL
2 parts light rum	2 parts strong	2 parts strong
¾ part simple syrup	¾ part sweet	1 part sweet
¼ part maraschino liqueur	¼ part sweet	
¼ part grapefruit juice	¼ part sour	1 part sour
¾ part lime	¾ part sour	

Pour all ingredients into a cocktail shaker with ice and shake for about fifteen seconds. Strain into a chilled cocktail glass.

"Papa" Hemingway always ordered a double serving, which is why this drink is also known as a Papa Doble. Many people leave out the simple syrup in this cocktail, so feel free to experiment and find what tastes good to you.

The Sweet Spot

While fruit is still a part of the sophisticated sips in this chapter, you can explore how other garden ingredients can heighten your cocktail pleasure. Flowers, herbs, and spices in sweet liqueurs and syrups either on their own or combined with light fruit flavors make for a sophisticated sweetness you won't be able to resist. With a smaller proportion of sweet, you'll need ingredients thicker than juice to give a smooth texture to your cocktail, so liqueurs and syrups will be your go-to sweets.

Some liqueurs we recommend include:

- Ginger
- Elderflower
- Green tea
- Lavender
- Peach
- Apricot
- Vanilla
- Chai
- Crème de violette (violet liqueur)
- Galliano (herb liqueur)
- Maraschino
- Crème de rose (rose liqueur)

maraschino vs. cherry liqueur

Maraschino liqueur doesn't taste at all like those sweet and waxy neon cherries that garnish many cocktails. Made with the flesh and ground pits of Marasca cherries, maraschino liqueur is bittersweet with a nutty flavor. It's distinct from cherry liqueurs like cherry Heering or crème de kirsch, which are sweeter and made with black cherries. Maraschino is also different from kirschwasser, a cherry brandy. Go back and check out our maraschino cherry recipe in Chapter 4, "Homemade Cocktail Garnishes," if you want to make a cocktail garnish that tastes great but doesn't glow in the dark.

Crème de violette used to be an integral part of a well-stocked bar. Then it disappeared for decades, relegating some vintage cocktails into obscurity and forcing others to adapt and evolve. The Aviation can be made without the lovely violet liqueur, but we're very glad that crème de violette is back on the scene so we can add its fragrance and purple tint to this once-forgotten drink.

Aviation

INGREDIENTS	RATIO	TOTAL
2 parts gin	2 parts strong	2 parts strong
¾ part maraschino liqueur	¾ part sweet	1 part sweet
¼ part crème de violette	¼ part sweet	
1 part lemon juice	1 part sour	1 part sour

Pour all ingredients into a cocktail shaker with ice and shake for about fifteen seconds. Strain into a chilled cocktail glass. *Optional:* Garnish with maraschino cherry.

Of course, you could pass over liqueur for a syrup instead. Whether you make it or buy it, these flavors of syrup are lovely in an Elegant Sips cocktail:

- Hibiscus
- Pomegranate
- Honey-lavender
- Lavender
- Lemon-basil
- Raspberry
- Rhubarb

- Strawberry-rhubarb
- Chamomile-mint
- Green tea

You know who likes flowers? Bees. And you know what we like? Their sweet, sweet honey. You don't need liqueur to add sugar flavor to your elegant cocktail. A simple honey syrup will do the job in its own way. If you want to get fancy, make the Honey-Lavender Syrup from Chapter 10, "DIY Gourmet." It's the cat's pajamas!

Bee's Knees

INGREDIENTS	RATIO
2 parts gin	2 parts strong
1 part honey syrup*	1 part sweet
1 part lemon juice	1 part sour

Pour all ingredients into a cocktail shaker with ice and shake for about fifteen seconds. Strain into a chilled cocktail glass. *Optional:* Garnish with a lemon spiral.

*Honey Syrup

▸ 1 part water
▸ 1 part honey

Mix together warm water and honey. No need to boil unless you're adding other flavors to the mix.

Playing with the Ratio: What If I Want a Sweeter Cocktail?

Herbs and flowers are sweet, but not as sweet as fruits and sugar. You might find that some experiments result in a flavor so subtle that the sour or strong part of your cocktail takes over. You won't count on sugar as much as you did in the Life of the Party chapter, so in some cases you might want to bump up the sweet part of your Elegant Sips ratio a little. Here's a gorgeous floral cocktail to try.

Delft Blue

Delft Blue

INGREDIENTS	RATIO	TOTAL
2 parts Genever gin	2 parts strong	2 parts strong
1 part crème de violette	1 part sweet	1½ parts sweet
½ part elderflower liqueur	½ part sweet	
1 part lemon juice	1 part sour	1 part sour

Pour all ingredients into a cocktail shaker with ice and shake for about fifteen seconds. Strain into a chilled cocktail glass. *Optional:* Drop some violets in the glass.

The Strong Stuff

Like the Life of the Party ratio, the beauty of Elegant Sips drinks is that you can basically use any spirit. Gin,

which can be a challenge to pair with the fruit-heavy cocktails that dominate the Life of the Party ratio, is perfect for the botanical flavors and strong citrus in this chapter. Clear spirits that don't have the deep flavors and sweet undertones of darker liquors are easy to pair, but the flexibility of this ratio makes it just as simple to match the character in more aged spirits. Besides the usual suspects, here are some liquors recommended for these drinks.

Apple Brandy

The American version is called *applejack* and the French version *calvados*. Both versions are brandy that has been freeze-distilled from apples. Not to be confused with brandy that has been infused or flavored with apples, it's actually quite strong. It's similar to bourbon and Cognac, only with a more intense heat and a dry apple finish that is reminiscent of an unsweetened hard cider. Apple brandy lacks honey or the oak notes of whiskey or oak-aged brandies. Laird's is the top-selling applejack, and you'll see calvados under brands such as Menorval, Morice, and Busnel.

The Jack Rose is perhaps the best-known applejack-based cocktail. Don't let its pinkish color and touch of sweetness fool you—this ain't no sissy cocktail.

Jack Rose

INGREDIENTS	RATIO	TOTAL
2 parts applejack	2 parts strong	2 parts strong
¾ part simple syrup	¾ part sweet	1 part sweet
¼ part grenadine	¼ part sweet	
1 part lime juice	1 part sour	1 part sour

Pour all ingredients into a cocktail shaker with ice and shake for about fifteen seconds. Strain into a chilled cocktail glass. *Optional:* Drop some violets in the glass.

Genever-Style Gin

Remember, genever-style gin doesn't taste like London gin, also known as *dry gin*. Sometimes called Holland or Dutch gin, it's slightly sweet with citrus and mild floral notes. There's no intense juniper flavor. Among the labels available are Bols, Damrak, Boomsma, and Zuidam.

Rhum Agricolle

Rhum agricole, made with cane sugar instead of molasses, has a stronger flavor and thicker mouthfeel than rum. It's a perfect match for a recipe that uses hibiscus syrup, which is similar to grenadine but has a floral twist. We didn't make our own syrup for this one; instead we found hibiscus flowers in syrup, which provided us with a sweet cocktail ingredient and a beautiful garnish all in one.

Hibiscus Flash

INGREDIENTS	RATIO	TOTAL
1 part white rhum agricole	1 part strong	2 parts strong
1 part white rum	1 part strong	
½ part hibiscus syrup	½ part sweet	1 part sweet
½ part simple syrup	½ part sweet	
1 part lime	1 part sour	1 part sour

Pour all ingredients into a cocktail shaker with ice and shake for about fifteen seconds. Strain into a chilled cocktail glass. *Optional:* Drop in a hibiscus flower from the syrup.

Sour Power

Lemon and lime are the classic choices for an Elegant Sips ratio. But with less sweetness to balance, sometimes they can be a little intense. Reducing the amount of lemon or lime and adding a little grapefruit or orange juice to the sour part of your ratio can keep your cocktail from becoming too tart. You may want to skip lemon and lime altogether and go straight to the grapefruit—it complements floral and herbal flavors delicately while still providing acidity.

Here's a recipe we made using fresh, pink grapefruit as the sour.

Barbados Rose

INGREDIENTS	RATIO	TOTAL
2 parts light rum	2 parts strong	2 parts strong
½ part falernum	½ part sweet	1 part sweet
½ part rose nectar	½ part sweet	
1 part grapefruit juice	1 part sour	1 part sour

Pour all ingredients into a cocktail shaker with ice and shake for about fifteen seconds. Strain into a chilled cocktail glass. *Optional:* Garnish by floating rose petals on the surface of the drink.

Using Homemade Ingredients

All sorts of goodies from the garden, farmers' market, and produce aisle can be a part of your Elegant Sips cocktails. Combine the spirit of the past and the modern love affair with market-fresh ingredients in your cocktails.

Home-Infused Sprits

You can tease the senses with subtle infusions and strong herbal flavors you might have been reluctant to try before you got a little practice. Here's a handful of infusions perfect for Elegant Sips:

- Chamomile dry gin
- Green tea genever gin
- Fennel vodka
- Apricot scotch
- Rhubarb white rum
- Cinnamon vodka
- Tomato gin
- Cucumber gin
- Pineapple gold rum
- Ginger vodka
- Lemon-basil vodka
- Strawberry tequila
- Cilantro-lime white rum

Rhubarbra Streisand

Rhubarb's distinct flavor prompted us to run through the other market-fresh ingredients with unique flavors like wild fennel. This fennel-infused vodka is pleasant but intense, so we had to play with the ratio a bit on this little pink number until we found the right balance.

Rhubarbra Streisand

INGREDIENTS	RATIO	TOTAL
2 parts fennel-infused vodka*	2 parts strong	2 parts strong
2 parts rhubarb syrup**	2 parts sweet	2 parts strong
½ part rhubarb juice	½ part sour	1½ parts sour
1 part lime juice	1 part sour	

Pour all ingredients into a cocktail shaker with ice and shake for about fifteen seconds. Strain into a chilled cocktail glass. *Optional:* Garnish with a sprig of fennel.

*Fennel-Infused Vodka

- ▶ 1 cup vodka
- ▶ 1 sprig fresh fennel (the greenery, not the bulb)

Follow instructions for Infused Spirit in Chapter 3, "Home-Infused Spirits." Taste after one day, since herbs release flavors quickly and you may be happy with the taste sooner than you think.

**Rhubarb Syrup

- ▶ 1 part water
- ▶ 1 part chopped rhubarb (stalk only)
- ▶ 1 part sugar

Follow instructions for Flavored Syrup in Chapter 5, "Homemade Flavored Syrup and Soda."

We were inspired to pair a soft peach liqueur with a bold infusion. Peach schnapps, which is a higher-proof and stronger-flavored peach liqueur, is too overpowering in this drink, so we recommend a lighter liqueur, such as Mathilde peach. Cinnamon and peach contrast and complement each other, making for a complex and satisfying drink with a little oomph.

Peach Sin

INGREDIENTS	RATIO
2 parts cinnamon vodka*	2 parts strong
1 part peach liqueur	1 part sweet
1 part lemon juice	1 part sour

Pour all ingredients into a cocktail shaker with ice and shake for about fifteen seconds. Strain into a chilled cocktail glass. *Optional:* Garnish with a peach slice or cinnamon stick.

*Cinnamon-Infused Vodka

▸ I cup vodka

▸ 5 cinnamon sticks, broken in half

Follow the instructions for Infused Spirit in Chapter 3, "Home-Infused Spirits." Let the cinnamon steep in the jar for two days, but taste it after one to ensure you don't end up with a flavor more intense than you'd like.

Homemade Syrups

Previous chapters have given you practice making flavored syrup by boiling equal parts of fruit, sugar, and water. You'll still want to do that for many of your Elegant Sips, but you can also try syrups that add a different kind of flavor to your cocktail. Here are some unique syrups you can experiment with:

- Rose
- Earl Grey tea
- Green tea
- Violet
- Orange zest and mint
- Lemon zest and basil
- Grapefruit zest and chamomile

- Hibiscus tea
- Lavender
- Apple and sage
- Almond and orange blossom
- Pear and rosemary
- Lemon verbena and strawberry

Tea syrup is sweet and fragrant. This gentle mix of green tea and lemon juice is perfect for sipping on a starry night.

Green Mar-tea-ni

INGREDIENTS	RATIO
2 parts vodka	2 parts strong
I part green tea syrup*	I part sweet
I part lemon juice	I part sour

Pour all ingredients into a cocktail shaker with ice and shake for about fifteen seconds. Strain into a chilled cocktail glass.

*Green Tea Syrup

▸ 1 part water

▸ 1 part sugar

▸ 1 green tea bag

Bring the water and sugar to a boil. Then reduce heat and add the green tea bag. Let simmer for five minutes and then turn off heat. Leave the bag steeping for an additional ten minutes. Remove bag and store syrup in a glass container in the refrigerator.

Homemade Liqueur Substitutes

If the liqueurs in the store aren't adventurous enough for you, make your own. Throw in some herbs and edible flowers while you're at it. Small batches—rather than using entire 750-milliliter bottles—will let you be bold in your experiments. Also, a variety of eight-ounce bottles of liqueurs lets you add variety without breaking the bank on obscure store-bought liqueurs you'll use only a handful of times.

Here are some fun flavor combinations to try in homemade liqueur substitutes:

- Pear and cinnamon
- Meyer lemon and vanilla
- Raspberry and basil
- Mint and apple
- Ginger and cranberries

When combining fruits and herbs, keep in mind that herbs release their flavor a lot faster. So if you're not cooking the herbs as part of your syrup, add them later in the steeping process.

Ditch the Recipe— Use the Ratio

With tea's growing popularity in the mixology world and our success in turning it into a fragrant syrup, we got curious about how it would taste in an infusion. Many gin makers are using a variety of teas in some of their gin offerings, and we can see why. Chamomile tea provides a nice counterpoint to gin's strong character and bold botanical flavors. Check out this ridiculously easy home infusion in action.

Chamoflage

INGREDIENTS	RATIO	TOTAL
2 parts chamomile-infused gin*	2 parts strong	2 parts strong
½ part ginger liqueur	½ part sweet	1 part sweet
½ part simple syrup	½ part sweet	
1 part lemon	1 part sour	1 part sour

Pour all ingredients into a cocktail shaker with ice and shake for about fifteen seconds. Strain into a chilled cocktail glass.

*Chamomile-Infused Gin

▶ 1 cup dry gin

▶ 1 chamomile tea bag

Let the tea bag steep in the gin for an hour. Remove the bag, squeezing it to extract the gin it soaked up, and store your infusion as you would any other spirit.

DIY *Gourmet*
homemade blackberry-blueberry-mint liqueur substitute

▶ ½ cup water

▶ ½ cup sugar

▶ 1 ½ cups blackberries and blueberries

▶ 2 mint leaves

▶ ¾ cup Cognac

Set half a cup of fruit in a glass jar and set aside. Combine water, sugar, and the remaining fruit mixture in a saucepan with the mint leaves. Bring to a boil. Cook for about three minutes. Let cool and then strain out and discard the solids. Refrigerate the syrup until cool. Pour the cooled syrup and the Cognac into the glass jar with the fruit. Seal the jar and shake the mixture. Steep for one to five days, shaking once a day. Strain out the fruit through an ultra-fine mesh strainer or cheesecloth. Store in a bottle as you would any other liqueur. Refrigeration isn't necessary.

How Did We Do That?

We wanted a subtle cocktail that opened up as you drank it. While we love fruit flavors, the idea behind this drink was to concentrate on the essence of herb and spice, so there are no sweet fruits and no lemon garnish. Here's a look behind the scenes on this one:

2 PARTS STRONG Chamomile is a gentle yet fragrant tea that soothes the senses. It calms some of gin's harsher notes without making it lose the intensity we love. While we never recommend using harsh or bottom-shelf spirits, a chamomile infusion tames a good gin that might just be a little too in-your-face for your tastes.

I PART SWEET Ginger liqueur is sweet and spicy—just the spark that this gentle-flavored spirit needs. We didn't want the ginger to take over, so we included just enough to let it shine through and then used simple syrup for additional sweetness.

I PART SOUR Lemon with our tea? That one's a no-brainer.

Your Turn

Grab that shaker, because it's time to concoct your own elegant masterpiece. We don't need to tell you what you like, so think about the flavors you want to experiment with. Then ask yourself questions that will help you create a drink like the Chamoflage:

- What flavor do I want to be the star of the show?
- How do I want to get that flavor into my cocktail? Infuse a spirit or make a syrup?
- What other flavor will enhance what I like about my main flavor?
- What will contrast this flavor without overpowering it?
- How will sour change the way my flavors interact?

The Flavor Profile Chart in the Appendix will give you plenty of suggestions for flavor pairings. Always sample ingredients separately before mixing to ensure that the quality is up to your standards. Mix a mini cocktail as a sample to get an idea of how to balance your chosen flavors.

Adjusting Your Elegant Sips Cocktail

This is one of the more forgiving ratios, but every ingredient is different, so a little adjustment might be needed to achieve the balance that separates a fine cocktail from an alcoholic mishmash. Here are some tips for tweaking your drink to perfection:

TOO STRONG? Try another splash of your sweet—or maybe even simple syrup or triple sec. There's plenty of sour in this drink, so adding more isn't going to help if it's too strong. If you know that your sweet is just the way you want it, then maybe a splash of water or club soda will do the job.

TOO SOUR? You could try some of the same techniques you'd use if the drink was too strong. Another option if it's only a little too sour is to add a splash of a less tart citrus such as orange juice or a little bit of another fresh juice.

TOO SWEET? This is unlikely considering the proportion of citrus, but when you're experimenting with the ratio or new ingredients, you might end up with something too sweet. Do more with less and try a dash or two of bitters. You probably don't want any more sour.

TOO BITTER? Although we're not using bitter ingredients, some herbs can add a touch of bitterness. Try a splash of simple syrup. Sour will make it even more bitter, so don't try more citrus.

TOO WEAK? Liquor is the only thing you can add to make it stronger, but do so slowly and carefully.

I FEEL PRETTY, OH SO PRETTY

GARNISHING WITH FLOWERS

Edible flowers are a fun way to dress up your cocktail. Although you won't actually be eating the flowers, dropping one or two colorful blooms in a drink or on the side of a glass takes only seconds and can look far more festive than a sprig of mint or slice of fruit. Check with a florist or local master gardener to make sure the flowers you choose are nontoxic if you're not sure. Here are some beauties ready for their cocktail close-up:

- Hibiscus
- Gardenia
- Jasmine
- Lavender
- Lilac
- Violet
- Pansy
- Snapdragon
- Sweet pea
- Nasturtium
- Rose
- Apple blossom
- Vanilla orchid

Edible Flowers

RATIO:
Varies

•

FLAGSHIP COCKTAILS:
Collins, Fizz, Mojito, Buck,
Champagne Cocktail

Effervescence

10

Cocktails made with club soda, ginger ale, or sparkling wine are refreshing and fun. Everyone loves bubbles! All these effervescent drinks are easy to jazz up with fresh fruit, herbs, and homemade ingredients. If you see wild blackberries growing on the side of the road, pick a basket and muddle some of them into a classic Mojito. Have some kumquat syrup left over from one of your cocktail creations? Use it in place of simple syrup in a Tom Collins. Add even more sweet fruits to your Mule and temper the extra sweetness with a few dashes of homemade cherry bitters.

Why It Works

These cocktails build on a concept you learned in Chapter 5: Adding a sparkling element can transport flavor in a unique and refreshing way. Tiny bubbles grab subtle tastes of your drink and percolate them to the surface. Sometimes the effervescence will tame a spirit's heat, while other times it will add a touch of elegance. Whether you're using bright club soda, your favorite ginger beer, or a fine sparkling wine, you'll enjoy how flexible and easy going these Effervescent ratios can be.

Tools of the Trade: Soda Siphon

Before the soda guns you see in bars today became the norm, bartenders used soda siphons to make seltzer or club soda. In old slapstick comedies, these pressurized bottles with spouts were an endless source of shenanigans. Countless cowboys were knocked to the floor by a stream of carbonated water sprayed at them by hapless barkeeps. The slick modern version uses CO_2  cartridges to add bubbles to the water, so you can make soda as you need it. They cost anywhere from fifty to one hundred dollars, but then you won't have to deal with plastic bottles (and the trash they make) or flat leftover soda since soda siphons carbonate as much as you need when you need it.

Playing It by Ear . . . with a Little Help

This whole book encourages sipping, adjusting, and personalizing as you mix, but with effervescent cocktails this step is even more important. Inconsistency in actual glassware sizes (e.g., sixteen-ounce Collins glasses and Champagne flutes the size of buckets) makes it smart to think about the proportions of your drink ahead of time, pour slowly, and taste often to get the right balance for that specific amount. The good news is that effervescent drinks are easy to adjust. They're larger than a typical cocktail, leaving more room for incremental mixing and mistake fixing.

The size of the glass is such an integral part of these types of cocktails that most recipes don't even tell you how much of an effervescent ingredient to add; they simply instruct you to top off until the glass is filled. If you

plan to use the "right" kind of glassware, the exact measurements listed for each ingredient will give you a way to better estimate how much of a sparkling ingredient you should use to top off. If you want to make drinks of different sizes—correct glassware be damned—or mix these up in big batches, the ratios can be your guide. As always, if you like it more sweet, sour, strong, or sparkling, you can come up with your own version based on our guidelines.

Ratio in Action: Club Soda

RATIO Varies

With little flavor of its own, club soda brightens up a cocktail with bubbles and dilution. (For a refresher on the difference between carbonated waters, see Chapter 5, "Weak But Not Powerless.") Here's a rundown on a few types of drink that use your fizzy friend.

Collins

A Collins is made and served in a Collins glass. These tall, narrow glasses vary in size from ten to fourteen ounces. You should build all drinks of this style, pouring each ingredient into the glass one by one after you've added ice. Technically, a Collins requires lemon as the sour— but even the most pedantic mixologists won't fault you for using the name for versions made with lime or grapefruit. Well, maybe they would, but you'll be too busy enjoying your delicious cocktail to care.

Originally made with Old Tom gin, the Tom Collins is the definitive cocktail of this type. It's a shame that many bars use artificial mix instead of lemon and simple syrup or sugar.

Tom Collins

INGREDIENTS	RATIO
1½ ounces London dry gin	3 parts strong
1 ounce simple syrup	2 parts sweet
½ ounce lemon juice	1 part sour
4 ounces club soda (adjust to taste)	8 parts weak

Fill a Collins glass with ice and pour in all ingredients, one at a time. *Optional:* Garnish with an orange slice.

Take the club soda out of the equation, and you'll notice that the Tom Collins is made with the Life of the Party ratio—3 parts strong, 2 parts sweet, and 1 part sour. A little effervescence gives that ratio an invigorating spin. Gin works well in this simple configuration, but it's so flexible you can use any spirit. This kind of drink just begs you to sip it outside on a warm summer day. The peachy version that follows includes slices of fresh fruit, which adds to the visual appeal and gives you a healthy snack to go with your cocktail.

Peach Collins

Peach Vodka Collins

INGREDIENTS	RATIO
1½ ounces vodka	3 parts strong
1 ounce peach syrup*	2 parts sweet
½ ounce lemon juice	1 part sour
4 ounces club soda	8 parts weak
Fresh peach slices	

Fill a Collins glass with ice and pour in all ingredients, one at a time. Slightly mash the peach slices and then place them in the drink. *Optional:* Garnish with mint.

*Peach Syrup

▸ 1 cup water

▸ 1 cup sugar

▸ 1 peach, sliced (We used super-sweet white peaches from the farmers' market.)

Follow the instructions for Flavored Syrup in Chapter 5, "Homemade Flavored Syrup and Soda."

The Paloma is a summer tequila cocktail that follows this model, using grapefruit soda instead of club soda and lime instead of lemon. We created a spiced-up, DIY version with ginger.

Ginger Paloma

INGREDIENTS	RATIO
1½ ounces silver tequila	3 parts strong
1 ounce ginger-grapefruit syrup*	2 parts sweet
½ ounce lime juice	1 part sour
4 ounces club soda	8 parts weak

Fill a Collins glass with ice and pour in all ingredients, one at a time. *Optional:* Garnish with a grapefruit slice.

*Ginger-Grapefruit Syrup

▸ 1 cup water

▸ 1 cup sugar

▸ ½ grapefruit, sliced (We like to use Ruby Reds for this one.)

▸ ¼ cup ginger, sliced and peeled

Bring all ingredients except the ginger to a boil. Then add the ginger and simmer for five minutes. Let the mixture cool, and then let it sit in the pan and steep for an additional ten minutes. Strain the solids and refrigerate the syrup.

Fizz

A Fizz is traditionally served in a highball glass, which is an eight- to ten-ounce glass similar to a Collins glass. You could also use a double

Old Fashioned glass, which is about the same size but is bucket shaped. Instead of building this drink over ice, shake your strong, sweet, and sour ingredients with ice and then strain the mixture into the glass. Whether or not the glass contains ice is up to you, but if it does, it would be less than what's in a Collins. Top off with club soda, and you have yourself a Fizz. As you'll see later in this chapter, you can include egg whites in a Fizz to add a sophisticated smoothness to your cocktail. For more particulars on how to make egg whites work smoothly and safely in your drink, just skip ahead to the "Advanced Mixology" section.

The Gin Fizz is like a smaller Tom Collins—with half as much club soda, and little or no ice. It also uses the Life of the Party ratio as its base.

Gin Fizz

INGREDIENTS	RATIO
1½ ounces London dry gin	3 parts strong
1 ounce simple syrup	2 parts sweet
½ ounce lemon juice	1 part sour
2 ounces club soda	4 parts weak

Shake all ingredients except club soda in a shaker filled with ice. Strain into a highball glass and top off with club soda. *Optional:* Put two or three ice cubes in the glass before straining the drink into it.

We just adore crème de violette, the violet-flavored liqueur. It's delicate and floral, without being overly sweet. It works beautifully in the next Fizz variation.

Violet Fizz

INGREDIENTS	RATIO	TOTAL
1½ ounces London dry gin	3 parts strong	3 parts strong
½ ounce crème de violette	1 part sweet	2 parts sweet
½ ounce simple syrup	1 part sweet	
½ ounce lemon juice	1 part sour	1 part sour
2 ounces club soda	4 parts weak	4 parts weak

Shake all ingredients except club soda in a shaker filled with ice. Strain into a highball glass and top off with club soda. *Optional:* Put two or three ice cubes in the glass before straining the drink into it.

using egg whites

Most of the time, you try to prevent cocktails from foaming. One exception is a cocktail shaken with egg. The protein in the egg combines with the citric acid from sour ingredients to create a fluffy, stable foam filled with tiny bubbles. (This is different from the gritty, loose foam that can result from putting blended fruit into a sparkling cocktail.)

Egg whites add a silky texture that goes perfectly with invigorating bubbles. Including the yolk is less common, but it adds texture, richness, and color. Adding egg white to a Gin Fizz gives you this smooth creation. To get fancy, shake the egg white first without ice. The higher temperature produces a better foam. Be careful: when egg and citric acid combine, it produces carbon dioxide. This can build pressure and pop the top of a shaker.

Silver Fizz

INGREDIENTS	RATIO
1½ ounces London dry gin	3 parts strong
1 ounce simple syrup	2 parts sweet
¾ ounce lemon juice	1½ parts sour
¾ ounce egg white (1 egg white)	
2 ounces club soda	4 parts effervescence

Shake all ingredients except club soda in a shaker filled with ice. Shake as hard as you can for as long as a minute so ingredients can bond. Strain into a highball glass and top off with club soda.

Swap pisco in for the gin, add a few dashes of bitters, and it's a Pisco Sour. Replace the London dry gin with sloe gin for a sweeter Sloe Gin Fizz.

Fear of salmonella has made many bars, and their customers, shy away from drinks made with raw egg. The risk is very small—you're more likely to choke to death on your food than get salmonella from an egg. If you don't want to take any risks, pasteurized egg whites are available in cartons at most grocery stores, but raw eggs foam faster and better than pasteurized whites.

It's no secret we love bourbon, so we also conjured up this Kentucky-inspired Fizz.

Lexington Fizz

INGREDIENTS	RATIO
1½ ounces bourbon	3 parts strong
1 ounce lemon mint syrup*	2 parts sweet
½ ounce lemon juice	1 part sour
2 ounces club soda	4 parts weak

Shake all ingredients except club soda in a shaker filled with ice. Strain into a highball glass and top off with club soda. *Optional:* Put two or three ice cubes in the glass before straining the drink into it.

*Lemon Mint Syrup

▸ ½ cup water
▸ ½ cup sugar
▸ Zest of one lemon
▸ Juice of one lemon
▸ 5 or 6 large mint sprigs

Bring sugar, water, and lemon zest to a boil. Then add mint. Simmer for five minutes. Let the mixture cool, and then let it sit in the pan and steep for an additional ten minutes. Strain the solids and refrigerate the syrup. Strain the solids, add the lemon juice, and refrigerate.

Strawberry Basil Mojito

Mojito

This Cuban cocktail is a favorite for experimentation. The original is made with muddled mint, rum, simple syrup, and lime juice built over ice in a highball or Collins glass and topped off with club soda. But once that muddler is out, other fruits and herbs can easily find their way into a Mojito. Here's our favorite recipe.

Mojito

INGREDIENTS	RATIO
3 mint leaves	
1½ ounces white rum	3 parts strong
1 ounce simple syrup	2 parts sweet
¾ ounce lime juice	1½ parts sour
4 ounces club soda	8 parts effervescence

Muddle the mint and simple syrup at the bottom of a highball or Collins glass. Add rum and lime juice. Then fill with ice and top off with club soda.

What better way to enjoy the delicious combination of strawberry and basil than in a gorgeous, fresh Mojito? Since lime is no longer the primary fruit, we reduced the amount of sour in this recipe to give more attention to the strawberry.

Strawberry Basil Mojito

INGREDIENTS	RATIO
3 basil leaves, torn	
3 strawberries, sliced	
1½ ounces white rum	3 parts strong
1 ounce simple syrup	2 parts sweet
½ ounce lime	1 part sour
4 ounces club soda	8 parts effervescence

Muddle the basil, strawberries, and simple syrup at the bottom of a highball or Collins glass. Add rum and lime juice. Then fill with ice. Top off with club soda.

Rum is part of what makes a Mojito a Mojito. But we grabbed the pisco and went nuts in the produce aisle for this next cocktail. Pisco has a stronger flavor than rum, so we amped up the sweet in this one.

Mango Cilantro Cooler

INGREDIENTS	RATIO
5 cilantro leaves	
1½ ounces pisco	3 parts strong
1½ ounces mango syrup* (do not discard the cooked fruit)	3 parts sweet
½ ounce lime juice	1 part sour
4 ounces club soda	8 parts effervescence

Muddle the cilantro and syrup at the bottom of a highball or Collins glass. Add a tablespoon of the cooked fruit from the mango syrup. Then add lime juice and pisco. Fill the glass with ice and top off with club soda.

*Mango Syrup

▶ 1 cup water
▶ 1 cup sugar
▶ 1 mango, peeled and chopped

Bring all ingredients to a boil and then simmer for five minutes. Let the mixture cool. Strain the solids and refrigerate the syrup. Keep the fruit you strained out for use in the cocktail.

Customizing the Collins, Fizz, and Mojito

You can make substitutions for any of the ingredients in these types of drinks. Oh, the freedom! Here are some suggestions:

USE A DIFFERENT SPIRIT. Mr. Collins's first name changes depending on which spirit you use. A John Collins is just a Tom Collins made with bourbon. Use tequila, and it's a Juan Collins. Ron Collins is a rum gent, while Ivan Collins is all about vodka. Dry gin is the typical Tom choice, but you could also try it with a genever-style gin or any other spirit. You may want to adjust the amount of sweet you use if your liquor has a sweet character.

TRY AN INFUSED SPIRIT. Any tasty infusion you dream up will taste great in a Collins and its cousins: fennel, cucumber, strawberry, peach, lavender . . . we could go on forever. Buy one off the shelves or make your own.

MAKE A FLAVORED SYRUP. Infused spirits aren't the only way to put exciting flavors into your sparkling drink. Making your own syrup is a simple method for adding ingredients such as mango, blueberry, lemon, and more.

PLAY WITH LIQUEUR. Whether you use only liqueur or a half-liqueur/half-syrup mixture for the sweet part of your cocktail, this opens a new world of flavors. If you use an herbal or an extra-sweet liqueur, you may need to make adjustments—either adding extra syrup or a couple dashes of bitters.

MUDDLE FRUIT AND HERBS. There's a whole spectrum of flavor in the garden and at the farmer's market, so mash it into your cocktail already. Taste the produce separately to decide if you need to adjust the amount of sweet ingredients you use. For example, with blackberries you may want to add a splash of simple syrup, while with tropical mangosteen you'll find you need less.

HAVE FUN WITH CITRUS. Lemons and limes are the easiest way to get sour flavor. For a less tart drink, try grapefruit. If you want a much sweeter drink, try orange or tangerine. You can even get crazy by mixing and matching.

the ice is right: making ice rings and blocks for punch

Keeping a big bowl of punch chilled can be tricky. You don't want to use standard ice cubes, because they will melt fairly quickly and water down your punch. The best way to keep your punch cold is with a large block of ice. All you need to do is fill a bundt cake pan or other deep, metal baking dish with water and freeze it. Put it in your punch, and you have a slow-melting way to keep the punch cool. You can also get a little fancy by suspending fruit or other garnishes in your ice ring or block. Here's how:

1. Arrange your fruit or other items along the bottom and sides of a large bundt cake pan or other deep, metal baking dish.
2. Fill it only partially with water, so that the fruit does not float around or gather in a clump.
3. Freeze the partially filled pan.
4. When the water is frozen, remove the pan and fill it to the top with additional water.
5. Freeze the pan again.
6. Remove pan from freezer and use warm water to loosen the ice from the pan.
7. Place ice ring in your punch and enjoy!

For your garnish, choose an item that is in the recipe or complements it. Suggestions for garnishes in your ice:

- Lemon and lime slices
- Raspberries
- Blackberries
- Cucumber slices
- Mint
- Watermelon
- Edible flowers

You can even freeze some of your punch as ice cubes or add juice or fruit to small ice cubes so they add fruit flavor over time.

DIY *Gourmet*
honey-lavender syrup

Floral and sweet, this syrup is a nice contrast to a crisp club soda or the dry sparkling wines you'll see in the next section of this chapter. We used good old clover honey (the kind that comes in the bear), but there are so many rich varieties of honey begging to make it into a drink. Lavender honey, blackberry honey, and orange honey all taste deep and delightful. Experiment with local honey when you can find it.

Lavender grows like crazy around our area, so we just plucked some and stuck it in our syrup. This would be a perfect addition to a Collins, Fizz, Champagne Cocktail, or a drink based on the Liquor Makes a Friend Ratio in Chapter 5.

Honey-Lavender Syrup

▸ 8 lavender tops (the flowers without the stem)
▸ 1 cup honey
▸ 1 cup water

Follow the instructions for Flavored Syrup in Chapter 5, "Homemade Flavored Syrup and Soda."

Ratio in Action: Champagne, Ginger Ale, or Ginger Beer

RATIO Varies

The effervescents can add more than just bubbles: These also add flavor. The mild, dry flavor of sparkling wine and the spicy yet sweet kick from ginger ale and ginger beer are delightful additions.

Champagne Cocktails

Champagne cocktails are an elegant way to turn an ordinary night into a special occasion. The classic version is made by dropping a sugar cube that has been soaked in Angostura bitters into a glass of sparkling wine and then topping it with a splash of Cognac. But there are no rules! Fruit, herbs, liquor, liqueurs, juices—they all can be part of the fabulousness. The French 75 that follows is a vintage jumping-off point for Champagne cocktail exploration.

French 75

INGREDIENTS	RATIO
1 ounce dry gin	2 parts strong
¾ ounce simple syrup	1½ parts sweet
½ ounce lemon juice	1 part sour
3 ounces sparkling wine	6 parts effervescence

Shake all ingredients except sparkling wine in a shaker filled with ice. Strain into a highball glass or large goblet and top off with sparkling wine. *Optional:* Garnish with lemon twist or spiral.

The French 75 is like a Tom Collins with sparkling wine instead of club soda. There's also a Champagne interpretation of another classic: the Hemingway Daiquiri. Although Hemingway might have wished this drink had a more masculine name, even he would have enjoyed downing the sparkling Papa's Twinkle cocktail.

Papa's Twinkle

INGREDIENTS	RATIO	TOTAL
½ ounce light rum	½ part strong	½ part strong
1 ounce grapefruit juice	1 part sour	1¼ parts sour
¼ ounce lime juice	¼ part sour	
¼ ounce simple syrup	¼ part sweet	½ part sweet
¼ ounce maraschino liqueur	¼ part sweet	
3 ounces sparkling wine	6 parts effervescence	6 parts effervescence

Shake all ingredients except sparkling wine in a shaker filled with ice. Strain into a tall Champagne flute or a large goblet and top off with sparkling wine. *Optional:* Garnish with a wedge of grapefruit.

You don't have to include a spirit. Champagne tastes great on its own, so a little bit of additional flavor from syrup, puree, liqueur, and juice could be just the thing. Here's a fragrant creation that's just made from syrup and sparkling wine, but it tastes like so much more is going on.

Washington Street Sparkler

INGREDIENTS	RATIO
1 ounce honey-lavender syrup*	1 part sweet
4 ounces sparkling wine	4 parts effervescence

Pour syrup into a Champagne flute and top off with sparkling wine. *Optional:* Garnish with a sprig of lavender on the stem.

*See instructions for Honey-Lavender Syrup in the DIY Gourmet section earlier in this chapter.

Another approach to making Champagne cocktails is to pour sparkling wine over liqueur, juice, or fruit puree. A Bellini is white peach puree topped with Prosecco, an Italian sparkling wine; a brunch wouldn't be brunch without a Mimosa—orange juice and Champagne; and a Kir Royale is a black currant liqueur called *crème de cassis* mixed with Champagne

Kir Royale

INGREDIENTS	RATIO
1 part crème de cassis	1 part sweet
5 parts sparkling wine	5 parts effervescence

Pour the crème de cassis into a Champagne flute and top off with sparkling wine.

Floral liqueurs are a natural match for dry sparkling wine. Crème de violette lends its beautiful purple color and delicate violet taste to a glass of Champagne. Top it off with a twist of lemon, and you have a sophisticated Champagne cocktail ready for any special occasion. The elderflower liqueur substituted in the following twist on a French 75 is another natural complement to Champagne.

French 76

INGREDIENTS	RATIO
¾ ounce elderflower liqueur	3 parts sweet
¼ ounce lemon juice	1 part sour
4 ounces sparkling wine	8 parts effervescence

Pour the liqueur and juice into a Champagne flute and top off with sparkling wine. *Optional:* Garnish with a lemon twist or spiral.

This cocktail puree of fresh currants was prepared using a different method from the one in Chapter 7, "Fresh Cocktail Puree." Because the skinned fruits are so tiny, cooking is more efficient than blending to remove the skins.

Currant Event

INGREDIENTS	RATIO
1 ounce red currant puree	1 part sweet
5 ounces sparkling wine	5 parts effervescence

Pour the puree into a Champagne flute and top off with sparkling wine. *Optional:* Add a squeeze of lemon. Garnish with a strand of red currants.

Effervescent ingredients mixed with an unstrained fruit mixture would make for a chunky, foamy cocktail. The bubbles would separate the puree instead of letting it blend with the other ingredients—that's why mixologists go through the trouble of straining. Don't tell the perfectionists, but we've made many cocktails for ourselves without making the extra effort to strain and have been happy with the results, even if they weren't very photogenic.

Cantaloupe is juicy and sweet, and we'd like to see it in more cocktails. For this next one, you can either throw in a mint leaf or two or top with a splash of mint liqueur.

The Minty Melon

INGREDIENTS	RATIO
1 ounce cantaloupe puree	1 part sweet
5 ounces sparkling wine	5 parts effervescence
1 splash of mint liqueur (such as peppermint schnapps)	5 parts effervescence

Pour the puree into a Champagne flute and top off with sparkling wine. Add a splash of mint liqueur to the top. *Optional:* Garnish with a cantaloupe ball and mint sprig speared on a toothpick.

Some liqueurs and purees are perfect partners with sparkling wine:

- Crème de violette
- Crème de cassis
- Blackberry liqueur or puree
- Peach liqueur or puree
- Raspberry liqueur or puree
- Strawberry liqueur or puree
- Rose liqueur
- Pear liqueur or puree
- Cranberry puree
- Cantaloupe puree
- Limoncello
- Lavender liqueur

A Wine, by any Other Name: Champagne, Sparkling Wine, Prosecco, and Cava

Yes, we know you know that true Champagne comes from the Champagne region of France. But when most people say *Champagne*, they mean sparkling wine in general. You'll see it under different names, depending on where it's made—Cava from Spain, Prosecco from Italy, and Espumante from Portugal, to name just a few. Have a fun tasting evening to find out the different regional styles!

There's no need to use expensive sparkling wine for mixing, but also steer clear of the super-cheap stuff. Low-end sparklers are often made by forcing carbonation rather than letting it occur naturally. The following phrases (and regional variations thereof) on the label mean that the bubbles weren't created artificially: Traditional Method, Methode Traditionelle, or Methode Champenoise.

The level of sweetness in the sparkling wine will dictate how it mixes with your other ingredients. Many sparkling wine producers include the French name for the sweetness category on the label or some other sort of indication of how dry or sweet it is.

By now you should be used to how confusing alcohol terminology can be, so it shouldn't come as a shock that the terms that designate how sweet the sparkling wine is are inconsistent. Here are some of the most common:

BRUT (AKA DRY) The most common style, this is the top choice for Champagne cocktails and what most people think of when they think "Champagne."

EXTRA DRY This one is in the middle of the sweetness scale. It's good for Champagne cocktails if you want to add a touch more sugar. Extra dry is actually *less* dry than brut—in other words, it's sweeter. But if you see "extra brut" be forewarned: It is not the same thing as extra dry Champagne.

SEC There's a hint of extra sweetness without losing the crispness looked for in sparkling wine. It's a little too sweet for some people's taste, but if you like a sweeter drink, go for it.

DEMI-SEC and **DOUX** These two are dessert-like in sweetness, and we don't recommend them for Champagne cocktails. But if you want to use them to make a dessert cocktail, who are we to stop you?

Buck or Mule

The only consistent thing about cocktail nomenclature and history is that it's often unclear. What started out as a Buck later became known as a Mule. No need to keep them straight, since they're two different names for the same thing—liquor mixed with citrus and ginger ale or ginger beer. In Chapter 5, you were introduced to the Moscow Mule, the cocktail many credit with changing what was previously known as a Buck into a Mule and making vodka a player on the cocktail scene. If you're confused, blame drunk people in Los Angeles, where the cocktail originated. The predecessor to the Moscow Mule was made with gin, like many of the signature drinks in this chapter traditionally were.

Here's a good one to try:

London Buck

INGREDIENTS	RATIO
1½ ounces London dry gin	3 parts strong
¾ ounce lemon juice	1½ parts sour
3 ounces ginger ale	6 parts effervescence

Fill a highball glass with ice and pour in all ingredients, one at a time.

The London Buck is a nice drink, but it's time to give it some fruit. Since we're adding some sweetness, let's go with the more robust ginger beer instead of ale and fuss with the ratio, bumping up the lemon to balance more sour against the sweetness.

ginger ale vs. ginger beer

Though once a barroom staple, ginger beer fell off the radar for a while— coming back around the same time as a thirst for cocktails from the 1940s, '50s, and '60s returned. Now it's relatively easy to find ginger beer alongside its more common cousin, ginger ale. Despite the *ale* and *beer* in their names, these sodas don't usually contain any alcohol. (There are a couple of brands of ginger beer that do.) Ginger ale is sweeter and slightly more carbonated, while ginger beer has more of the spicy kick associated with ginger.

Raspberry Buck

INGREDIENTS	RATIO	TOTAL
2 ounces bourbon	4 parts strong	4 parts strong
½ ounce simple syrup	1 part sweet	2 parts sweet
½ ounce raspberries (about 5)	1 part sweet	
1 ounce lemon juice	2 parts sour	2 parts sour
3 ounces of ginger beer	6 parts effervescence	6 parts effervescence

Muddle the raspberries, simple syrup, and lemon juice at the bottom of a highball glass. Add bourbon and ice. Then pour in ginger beer. *Optional:* Garnish with a lemon or speared raspberry.

The beauty of the Buck is you really can use any spirit you want. Here we gave silver tequila a spin, again bumping up the strong and sour to accommodate the fruit sweetness we added.

Jalisco Buck

INGREDIENTS	RATIO
2 ounces silver tequila	4 parts strong
1 ounce fresh lime juice	2 parts sour
1 or 2 large strawberries	1 part sweet
3 ounces ginger ale	6 parts effervescence

Muddle the strawberries and line juice at the bottom of a highball glass. Add tequila and ice, and top with the ginger ale. Garnish with a lime wedge. *Optional:* Use a salt rim.

Ditch the Recipe— Use the Ratio

There are lots of ratios to play with in this chapter and a cosmos of flavors to chose from. For your next cocktail adventure, we used the Collins ratio and subbed in sparkling wine for the usual club soda. This little twist gives the drink a little romance.

Nuts About You

INGREDIENTS	RATIO
1½ ounces dark rum	3 parts strong
1 ounce orgeat	2 parts sweet
½ ounce lemon juice	1 part sour
4 ounces sparkling wine (adjust to taste)	8 parts effervescence

Fill a Collins glass with ice and pour in all ingredients, one at a time. *Optional*: Garnish with a lemon spiral.

How Did We Do That?

The orgeat you made in Chapter 7's "Advanced Mixology" section isn't just for tropical drinks. The rich almond flavor is a good match for the light crispness of sparkling wine. Typically orgeat is mixed with other sweets, playing only a supporting role. The powerful nuttiness is a surprising sensory experience, and pairing it with bubbles in dry Champagne balances the intensity to give you a more sophisticated drinking experience. Here's what went into making this sparkling treat.

3 PARTS STRONG We chose dark rum because its deep and sweet flavor is a match of the flavor profile of orgeat, which we knew we wanted to use as our sweet.

2 PARTS SWEET Orgeat can be overpowering in some drinks if used as the primary sweet. However, effervescence is the dominant feature of this cocktail and the orgeat would be sufficiently diluted.

1 PART SOUR Lemon juice and sparkling wine complement each other. It's the best choice of citrus for an elegant drink, since lime juice can be brassy.

8 PARTS EFFERVESCENCE Using sparkling wine in a larger quantity than is typical for a Champagne cocktail adds more flavor than plain soda water. With the sweeter ingredients, we needed something dry like sparkling wine for balance.

Your Turn

By now you've got a good idea of what you like and why, but keep your eye on ways effervescence can improve upon combinations in your repertoire. Remember to create your drinks carefully, building and shaking ingredients as instructed so you don't lose the effervescence. And a tip for topping off with Champagne or other bubblies: Hold the glass at an angle and pour slowly down the side of the inside of the glass to avoid foaming and spilling.

Adjusting Your Effervescent Cocktail

In a bigger glass, there's more room to play with the proportions. However, you don't want to pour and pour until you end up needing a second glass. Taste as you go, and use these adjustment tips:

TOO STRONG? If you suspect a whole shot of liquor will be too strong for your tastes in this type of cocktail, try starting with less. Then, in increments, add more to taste. If you still end up with a drink that's too strong, slowly add some more effervescence in small amounts.

TOO SOUR? Add a splash of simple syrup. If that still doesn't float your boat, try a wee bit more effervescence.

TOO SWEET? A dash or two of bitters can do wonders to balance out a drink. It's a much easier and more reliable fix than monkeying with the sour. If you want more tartness, don't be afraid of a squeeze of citrus.

TOO WEAK? Adding more liquor is usually a last resort, but in the case of these cocktails, bumping up the alcohol content isn't as dramatic of a change as it would be in a smaller, less diluted drink. As always, when adding booze, do so slowly and taste often.

Notes

Notes

RATIO:
Varies

•

FLAGSHIP COCKTAILS:
Anything You Can
Dream Up!

Parties
and Punch

11

W hip out the pitcher and punch bowl, because it's party time! If you want to serve great cocktails to a roomful of people, you don't need to be stuck behind the bar all night. You can use the cocktail ratios you already know to make drinks by the pitcher instead of the glass, or you can come up with a whole new ratio by riffing on the punches we'll share with you in this chapter. The punch bowl is a flexible venue for experimentation. You can make it strong, fruity, spicy, sour—whatever you feel will be a crowd pleaser. Think of your punch in terms of ratios, and you'll be able to make punch in any quantity using the same recipe.

How to Batch Different Types of Drink

Before delving into punches, let's go over using the ratios you already know to make drinks in larger quantities. The pros call it *batching*. First, select the cocktail you wish to batch. Next, determine whether that drink is usually shaken, stirred, or built. Go through the categories that follow, pick the one that fits, and then read each batching method to see which one will work best for you and your party.

Drinks That Are Normally Stirred

Cocktails that are stirred are usually made with alcoholic ingredients of equal consistency—such as the gin and vermouth in a Martini. There are two ways to mix stirred drinks by the batch: the freezer method and the ice cube method. The freezer method is quicker, and it's well suited for large groups or situations where guests will be serving themselves. The ice cube method is more authentic, but it's also more time-consuming.

The Freezer Method

1. Stir ingredients together in a pitcher, adding the equivalent of one tablespoon of water for every three ounces of cocktail mixture.
2. Put the entire pitcher in the freezer for an hour.
3. When you're ready to serve, pour individual servings into chilled cocktail glasses.

The Ice Cube Method

1. Stir ingredients together in a pitcher and leave it at room temperature.
2. When you are ready to serve, fill a mixing glass most of the way with ice, pour in as much of your cocktail mixture as will fit, and stir.
3. Strain into chilled cocktail glasses.
4. Repeat this process until the pitcher is empty (usually three to five times).

TASTE BEFORE WASTE

Lemon and lime juice in large quantities can start to take over, even if you're using it in the same proportions you would in a single drink. First make the batch according to your usual single-serving ratio. Then taste it and add simple syrup until the flavor is balanced. You won't need very much of it, and you shouldn't need to do anything else. If you're making a huge amount—say for fifty people—you may want to add a little more liquor, too.

Drinks That Are Normally Shaken

There are also two ways to batch these cocktails—the faster way and the more authentic way. Drinks like the Margarita and Jack Rose, which have little juice and lightweight liqueurs or syrups, can be made with either the ice cube or shaker method. Tropical drinks like the Mai Tai and Bahama Mama require the shaker method so the many juices and syrups can bond together in a cohesive, smooth cocktail without separating. Note that some shaken drinks may not be right for batching; double-check the end of this section to see types of drinks we wouldn't batch.

The Ice Cube Method

1. Stir the ingredients together vigorously in a pitcher, leaving enough room to later add about a half pitcher's worth of ice.
2. Refrigerate until needed.
3. Add the ice three to five minutes before serving. Each glass should contain ice.

The Shaker Method

1. Stir the ingredients together vigorously in a pitcher.
2. When you are ready to serve guests, fill a shaker most of the way with ice, pour in the cocktail mixture, and shake.
3. Strain individual servings into chilled glasses—filled with ice, if appropriate.

Effervescent Drinks Normally Built over Ice

You don't want to mix a big pitcher of Mojitos, since it will lose carbonation pretty quickly and the muddled ingredients won't be distributed equally as you pour. However, there is a way to simplify serving effervescent drinks to a crowd—with or without muddled fruit and herbs.

1. **FIGURE OUT THE PROPORTION OF MIXED INGREDIENTS TO EFFERVESCENT TOP-OFF.** For instance, if your drink is three parts strong, two parts sweet, one part sour, and eight parts effervescence, that equates to three parts mixed ingredients for every four parts of effervescent.
2. **MAKE A SCALED-UP VERSION OF THE NON-SPARKLING PART OF YOUR** cocktail. Muddle any fruit and herbs in big batches and store the batches in the fridge.
3. **AS NEEDED, DOLE OUT INDIVIDUAL PORTIONS OF MIXED INGREDIENTS AND TOP OFF WITH ICE AND EFFERVESCENT.** Make sure to evenly distribute ingredients like herbs and fruit chunks.

Cocktails We Don't Recommend Batching

It's true: There are some drinks that don't play well in big numbers. You'll have to make the following types of drinks one at a time:

ANYTHING MADE WITH EGGS OR DAIRY. The ingredients are too thick and require a good, hard shake to get them to bond and create the proper texture.

DRINKS WHERE MUDDLED INGREDIENTS ARE SHAKEN AND THEN STRAINED. This two-step process of releasing flavor cannot be replicated by stirring.

GIN & TONIC AND OTHER LIQUOR MAKES A FRIEND COCKTAILS. There are only two ingredients and one of them is probably bubbly. Why would you mix a big batch of Rum & Coke when it's simple enough to pour on a one-off basis and carbonation is key?

THE OLD FASHIONED OR OTHER ORIGINAL COCKTAIL DRINKS. This is technically possible if you use simple syrup instead of a muddled sugar cube, but the high proportion of liquor requires more attention to detail and leaves no room for adjusting.

The Math Behind Batching

It's likely that the size of your pitcher dictates the size of one batch of cocktails. So while you can easily take your favorite single-serving recipe and multiply it by the number of drinks you want to make, you may need to work backwards to figure out how many drinks fit in your pitcher. For this example, let's say you wanted to make a thirty-ounce pitcher of Martinis.

Here's what you would do:

FIGURE OUT HOW MUCH ONE "PART" IS.

- Add up the total number of parts in the ratio. For the Martini: 4 parts + 1 part = 5 parts.
- Divide your desired batch size by the number of parts. The result will be the measurement you will use as one part when you mix your batch. In this example: 30 ounces per pitcher ÷ 5 parts per drink = 6 ounces. Therefore, one part equals six ounces for the purposes of mixing your batch of Martinis.

MULTIPLY EACH PART OF THE RATIO BY THE MEASUREMENT YOU'RE USING.

- 4 parts of gin × 6 ounces = 24 ounces of gin
- 1 part of dry vermouth × 6 ounces = 6 ounces of dry vermouth
- Total = 30 ounces

Packing a Punch (Cocktail)

Punch can be fruity, spiced, or something in between—and it doesn't have to come in a giant bowl. You can make it for one or for five hundred. A punch cocktail is just a drink with a higher proportion of juice and other light, no-alcohol or low-alcohol ingredients such as water, tea, club soda, ginger ale, and wine. It shouldn't be surprising that the Chapter 6 Life of the Party ratio—three parts strong, two parts sweet, one part sour—is the base of the most flexible punch ratio. What we're adding to that is four parts low- or no-alcohol mixer. To make things simple, we call these ingredients *weak,* the term we used for the fizzy waters in Chapter 5 and Chapter 10. So the first punch ratio we're going to play with is three parts strong, two parts sweet, one part sour, and four parts weak.

Classic Rum Punch

INGREDIENTS	RATIO
3 parts rum	3 parts strong
2 parts simple syrup	2 parts sweet
1 part lime juice	1 part sour
4 parts water	4 parts weak

Mix all ingredients and keep it chilled until serving time. *Optional:* To add a Caribbean flair, add spices.

Rum Punch inspired many variations that were popular centuries ago, and it remains the basis for many potent punches today. Fish House Punch dates back to late-eighteenth-century Philadelphia. Our recipe is an adaptation of this potent punch the Founding Fathers liked to knock back while, you know, building a nation.

Another variation is to use cold black tea for a portion of the weak ratio or to dilute with cold black tea such as Darjeeling if the recipe is too strong for your taste. Try coconut water in place of water to add a mild but unsweetened coconut flavor.

Fish House Punch

INGREDIENTS	RATIO	TOTAL
2 parts Jamaican rum	2 parts strong	3 parts strong
1 part Cognac	1 part strong	
½ part peach schnapps	½ part sweet	2 parts sweet
1½ parts simple syrup	1½ parts sweet	
1 part lemon juice	1 part sour	1 part sour
4 parts water	4 parts weak	4 parts weak

Mix all ingredients and keep it chilled until serving time.

For large batches: Place a large ice block in a punch bowl and pour the punch over it.

For an individual drink: Serve in a punch cup or an Old Fashioned glass with two large ice cubes.

Optional: Add thin slices of lemon to the punch bowl and top individual servings with a dash of grated nutmeg.

The Fish House and Tequila Fresa punches used the Life of the Party ratio as inspiration.

DIY *Gourmet*
sweet tea bourbon

If you can't find a bottle of this southern specialty in stores, you can always mix up a batch of your favorite sweet tea and make our own with this easy recipe.

Sweet Tea Bourbon

▸ 1 part sweet tea
▸ 4 parts bourbon

Combine tea and spirits.

Minty Southern Punch

INGREDIENTS	RATIO
4 parts sweet tea bourbon	4 parts strong
1 part lemon mint simple syrup	1 part sweet
1 part lemon juice	1 part sour
2 parts soda	2 parts weak
Lemon slices and fresh mint sprigs for garnish	

Combine the sweet tea bourbon with the other ingredients, except soda, in a punch bowl and stir. Add your ice block and the lemon slices and fresh mint. To help release the minty flavor, take the leaves in the palm of your hand and clap once before use. Serve in punch cups over ice. Adjust mint and soda to taste.

Maybe you want a punch that's a little sweeter than what George Washington gulped. With our Tequila Fresa Punch creation, we tweaked the Life of the Party–based punch ratio to make it taste less old-timey and more fruity. We used orange juice as a sweet to hang on to the citrus tang to keep it from getting too sugary.

Another flexible ratio is the one in the Elegant Sips chapter. The Red Berry Punch recipe turns it into a sophisticated gin punch. If you like a stronger punch, the Minty Southern Punch doubles the amount of liquor while leaving the rest of the Elegant Sips ratio untouched.

Tequila Fresa Punch

INGREDIENTS	RATIO	TOTAL
3 parts strawberry-infused reposado tequila*	3 parts strong	3 parts strong
1 part triple sec	1 part sweet	2½ parts sweet
1½ parts orange juice	1½ parts sweet	
1 part lime juice	1 part sour	1 part sour
4 parts grapefruit soda	4 parts effervescence/weak	4 parts effervescence/weak
1 dash orange bitters		
Sliced strawberries for garnish		

Mix all ingredients except soda and keep it chilled until serving time.

For large batches: Place a large ice block in a punch bowl and pour the punch over it. Float the fruit on top.

For an individual drink: Serve in a punch cup or an Old Fashioned glass with two large ice cubes. Or shake all ingredients (except fruits and soda) with ice. Serve with two or three large ice cubes in a goblet or double Old Fashioned glass.

*Strawberry-Infused Reposado Tequila

▸ 1 part reposado tequila
▸ 1 part chopped strawberries

Follow instructions for Infused Spirit in Chapter 3, "Home-Infused Spirits" and let mixture steep for five days.

Red Berry Punch

INGREDIENTS	RATIO
2 parts gin	2 parts strong
1 part raspberry syrup	1 part sweet
1 part orange-lemon juice mixture	1 part sour
2 parts club soda	2 parts weak
1 dash Sassy Red Bitters (see the recipe in Chapter 4, "Homemade Bitters")	
Raspberries, orange slices, and lemon slices for garnish	

Shake all ingredients (except fruits) with a lot of ice. Pour into tumbler with shaved or crushed ice and garnish with fruit and berries.

For large batches: Combine all ingredients except club soda. Place a large ice block in a punch bowl. Pour the punch over it and top with club soda. Float the fruit on top.

For an individual drink: Serve in a punch cup or an Old Fashioned glass with two large ice cubes.

If you're looking for a lighter punch with less liquor, try the Basil-Watermelon Lemonade. It's perfect for a summer barbecue. You can swap in tequila or vodka in place of the gin—or leave out the spirits altogether for a mildly flavored delight. It's more of a watermelon-ade than a lemonade, but that just didn't sound as snappy.

Basil-Watermelon Lemonade

INGREDIENTS	RATIO
4 parts gin	4 parts strong
4 parts basil-watermelon lemonade*	4 parts sweet
2 parts soda	2 parts weak
Fresh basil and watermelon slices for garnish	

Combine gin and basil-watermelon lemonade into a punch bowl. Then add an ice block. Ladle individual servings into punch cups over ice. Top with soda, basil, and watermelon slices.

*Basil-Watermelon Lemonade

- ▸ 1 cup watermelon
- ▸ 1 ounce lemon juice
- ▸ 1 ounce simple syrup
- ▸ 3 basil leaves

Muddle all ingredients. Once the watermelon releases most of its juices, strain out the solids and chill.

Sangria

Sangria is a DIY dream. It's a wine punch with fruit and liquor in it. What kind of wine, fruit, and liquor? That's up to you. Some people like to top their sangria off with ginger ale, lemon-lime soda, or club soda. Some people like it room temperature, while others drink it over ice. It's hard to find anyone who doesn't like sangria. It's possible they wouldn't be people worth knowing.

Using expensive wine is a waste, since any nuances in flavor will be obscured by the sugars and liquor. Don't use wine that has been left open for too long; it will have oxidized. Even though you're adding other things, wine is still the primary flavor in this punch, so you should like the one you use. You can make it with any kind of wine—red, white, rose, or sparkling. Dry wines without a lot of oak and tannin flavors are best. Brandies are the traditional choice for liquor, though rum tastes great, too. For the fruit, pick three or four that complement each other, and remember that sliced fruits release their flavor more quickly than whole fruits like blueberries or grapes, which are entirely protected by skin. Fruit juice, herbs, and spices can also liven up a wine punch.

Sangria

- ▸ I bottle red wine
- ▸ 2 ounces Cognac
- ▸ 2 ounces triple sec
- ▸ 2 ounces simple syrup
- ▸ 2 cups chopped fruit (if using citrus, cut in slices and leave the peel on)

Combine all ingredients and let them steep in the refrigerator for at least an hour and up to twelve hours. To serve, put a scoop of the fruit from the sangria in each cup. Then pour the punch. *Optional:* Top off each glass with one or two ounces of club soda, ginger ale, or lemon-lime soda.

If you use sparkling wine, don't open it until you're ready to serve. Instead, steep the rest of the ingredients together so the fruit can release its flavors. Then top off with the sparkling wine when you're ready to serve.

Here are some fruit combinations we love, but it's anything goes with sangria:

RED WINE

- Orange, lemon, apple
- Pineapple, orange, cucumber, and strawberries
- Fig and Bing cherry
- Peaches, blueberry, blackberry, and Meyer lemon

WHITE WINE

- Pineapple and mango
- Tangerine, grapefruit, watermelon
- Strawberry, raspberry, nectarine
- Pear, apple, orange, and apricot

Pisco Punch

When South Americans came to California during the Gold Rush, they brought a clear grape-based brandy called *pisco* with them. It became a popular ingredient in many San Francisco cocktails of the late nineteenth century, most famously Pisco Punch. There are many variations on this simple punch, which was created by the Bank Exchange saloon, since the owner took the original recipe with him to his grave. To be authentic, you should use gomme syrup—a rich

Pisco Punch

simple syrup made with gum arabic that adds a silky texture and prevents sugars from crystallizing. Most people just aren't going to bother to hunt for gum arabic in order to make gomme syrup at home, so we skipped it. The result is still fantastic and smooth.

Pisco Punch

INGREDIENTS	RATIO
2 parts pisco	2 parts strong
¾ parts pineapple-infused rich syrup*	¾ parts sweet
¾ parts lemon juice	¾ parts sour

Place a chilled pineapple chunk you saved from the syrup at the bottom of a coupe or punch cup. Shake the pisco, syrup, and lemon with ice. Then pour on top of the pineapple.

*Pineapple-Infused Rich Syrup

- ▶ 2 cups sugar
- ▶ 1 cup water
- ▶ ½ pineapple, cored and sliced into chunks

Bring the sugar and water to a boil. Let simmer for three minutes. Remove from heat and set aside to cool. Place the pineapple chunks in a large bowl and pour the cooled syrup over them. Cover and let it steep and chill overnight. Remove the pineapple chunks and save them to serve with the punch. You'll use one-quarter of a pineapple per cup of syrup; this recipe makes 2 cups.

Sparkling Punches

Champagne cocktails are fun and festive, so it follows that many great punches that are really just one giant Champagne cocktail. You don't want warm or flat sparkling wine, so be sure to chill it and add it just before serving. The simple punch that follows, made with Prosecco, is a lot of fun to customize. We made it with limoncello, an Italian sweet lemon liqueur

Italian Sparkling Citrus Punch

we think is a great match for Italian sparkling wine. Why not swap in orangecello? Now there are a whole host of "cellos" out there to use, even watermeloncello!

You'll probably want to use full bottles of Prosecco for a punch, so we included measurements based on that. However, you can easily turn the ratio into individual servings.

Italian Sparkling Citrus Punch

INGREDIENTS	RATIO	TOTAL
1 cup vodka	2 parts strong	2 parts strong
1½ cups simple syrup	1½ parts sweet	1½ parts sweet
1½ cups limoncello	1½ parts sweet	3 parts sweet
½ cup lemon juice	1 part sour	1 part sour
1 bottle Prosecco (750 milliliters, or just over 3 cups)	6 parts effervescence/ weak	6 parts effervescence/ weak

Stir all ingredients except the Prosecco together in a glass punch bowl. Cover and refrigerate for two hours. Add the Prosecco and an ice block just before serving.

This same formula lets you create a floral punch that's not too sweet, thanks to the deep flavors in Cognac and maraschino liqueur. We used tangerine as our sour, since it provides the acidity we needed for balance but has a sweeter flavor than lemon, lime, or grapefruit. If you want it less sweet, you can always use orange or include lemon juice as part of your sour. Lavender liqueur swapped in for the elderflower liqueur is another scented sweet we recommend.

Flower Power Punch

INGREDIENTS	RATIO	TOTAL
1 cup Cognac	2 parts strong	2 parts strong
¼ cup maraschino liqueur	½ part sweet	3 parts sweet
1¼ cups elderflower liqueur	2½ parts sweet	
½ cup tangerine juice	1 part sweet citrus, functioning as sour	1 part sweet citrus, functioning as sour
1 bottle sparkling wine (750 milliliters, or just over 3 cups)	6 parts effervescence/ weak	6 parts effervescence/ weak

Stir all ingredients except the sparkling wine together in a glass punch bowl. Cover and refrigerate for two hours. Add the sparkling wine and an ice block just before serving.

The flavors that make great individual drinks also make great batches of drinks and punches. The same balancing principles you use when mixing for yourself apply when making a giant bowl of punch or an enormous batch of cocktails. Make yourself a single-serving version before moving on to the high-volume version.

Adjusting Your Punches and Batches

There's more room to play with the proportions when you're making drinks by the gallon. But there's no reason to pour random ingredients in until you end up with something that resembles frat house jungle juice more than it does a balanced cocktail. Make small testers for experimentation purposes, and taste as you go. Here are some adjustment guidelines to help you.

TOO STRONG? Start off with half to three quarters as much liquor as you think you'll need and adjust up incrementally. If it's still too strong but the consistency and rest of the flavors are pleasing, top off with a little more of your weak ingredient. A splash of simple syrup can often fix a punch that's too sharp.

TOO SOUR? Apply the same guidelines for adjusting the strong part of your ratio. A splash of weak or sweet can do the trick.

TOO SWEET? Try a dash or two of bitters. If you find it lacking in tartness, squeeze in more citrus.

TOO WEAK? You may actually have added too much of your weak ingredient. If you can't balance this with a splash of simple syrup or sour, then carefully add a splash or two of your spirit.

Notes

_____

_____

_____

_____

_____

_____

_____

_____

_____

_____

_____

_____

APPENDIX
Flavor Profile Chart

The Flavor Profile Chart is your source for cocktail ingredient gossip. Find out which ingredients are in love, which ones can't stand each other, which ones will behave only in front of a chaperone, and which ones secretly long to be in a threesome with a bitter liqueur and a sprig of mint. We took a whole host of common and not-so-common ingredients and categorized them according to how they perform in a cocktail.

What This Chart Will Do for You

Sure, a peach is sweet . . . but how sweet is it in comparison to an apple or rambutan, and will you need to add sugar if you swap one for the other? Maybe you love cilantro and want to figure out if it gets along with your favorite spirit, bourbon. (It doesn't.)

Or perhaps you've just made a wicked pineapple syrup and now you want to know what to pair it with. (Try pisco or basil.) When you're ready to make some pairing decisions, this chart will help you out.

The chart contains extremely general information intended to help you brainstorm cocktails. So when you read about ingredients like tomatoes, Cognac, and limes, you'll see basic terms; you won't see information on how Early Girl tomatoes compare with Heirloom tomatoes, whether Hennessy or Remy Martin will taste better in your punch, or why the fruit from your Aunt Bessy's tree is more tart than the citrus at Whole Foods. The ingredients are arranged by taste categories from sour to sweet and everything in between. We assume you will taste things yourself to test quality and compatibility before using them, but here are some tips on how to choose what goes into your drinks.

Spirits and Liqueurs

Although we're not specifying which brand names you should buy, remember that brands do differ. Each producer has a unique process that adds character to the overall profile of the spirit. And in most cases, price matters. Yes, there are plenty of twenty-dollar bottles that can kick the fancy behinds of spirits that are two or three times that, but if it comes in a plastic jug and costs five dollars a gallon, you'll probably get what you pay for (and maybe a hangover to go with it). You're accenting the flavor of spirits we enjoy with fresh ingredients, not hiding the taste of cheap hooch. It can't be said enough: Taste your spirit alone before you mix with it so you can understand the underlying flavors you'll be matching and complementing.

Herbs

With the exception of teas, the herbs you use should be fresh and not dried. Remember to muddle them gently and take care when using them in infusions since they release flavor quickly and easily.

Citrus Juice

When a recipe calls for lemon juice, lime juice, or any citrus juice, fresh-squeezed is your best bet for the best taste. Even high-end, organic juices taste very different from the home-squeezed stuff. Most of these fruits are widely available across different time zones and climates year round. So unless you can't find it or the crop in your area is inferior, reach for the juicer instead of the bottle.

Be sure to choose ripe fruit and add the juice slowly to account for variations. If you want to keep a bottle of the commercial stuff on hand, taste it side by side with fresh so you'll know how to compensate for any difference in flavor. You can juice ahead of time and store for future use. Many bartenders swear that four-hour-old lime juice is better than just-squeezed. We're not sure about that, but you should be aware that the juice may taste a little different if it's been sitting around.

Fruits and Vegetables

Only use ripe fruit. If you don't know how to tell, ask the grocer or grower. Seasonal and local is best, but we're not the food police. If you're able to garden, do it! Even if all you have is a little mint plant, there's nothing like plucking a fresh leaf from your own plant when you are mixing up a cocktail. As you decide to juice, muddle, or cook the produce, think about how quickly and easily the fruit or vegetable releases its flavor, and identify the tastiest way to experience it. Apples juice well but are terrible for muddling because of their fibrous texture and light flavor. On the other hand, juicing a mango is probably a waste of your time when chopping it up or pureeing it already releases so much liquid.

Syrups and Purees

Earlier chapters list general guidelines for syrup and purees, but you'll probably adjust each one you make based on how sweet the fruit or herb is and how much of it you put in. Prepared syrups and purees are decent stand-ins, especially if the fruit is one that's hard to find, like passion fruit or guava. There are plenty of artisan brands that use natural ingredients, and they can be time savers. Compare your stuff to the ones the pros make to see what you can do differently (or what you're doing better).

The Flavor Profile Chart

Category	Ingredient	Other Characteristics	Method to Make It Cocktail-Ready	Friends
sour	grapefruit	mild sweetness	syrup, juice, muddle, infuse	Campari, Champagne, coconut, gin, vodka, ginger, triple sec, honey, lemon, lime, melon, mint, oranges, papaya, pineapple, pomegranate, raspberries, strawberries, vanilla
sour	kumquats	mild bitterness	puree, muddle	cranberries, strawberries, cinnamon, coconut, ginger, honey, lemon, lime, mango, mint, oranges, papaya, persimmons, pineapple, pomegranate, rum, vodka, vanilla
sour	lemons	true sour citrus	juice, infuse, muddle, liqueur	*Everything!*
sour	limes	true sour citrus	juice, infuse, muddle	*Everything!*
sour	oranges	moderately sweet	juice, muddle, infuse, liqueur	*Everything!*
sour	rhubarb	herbal	syrup, juice, infuse	apples, raspberries, strawberries, cinnamon, oranges, lemon, lime, ginger, triple sec, gin, vodka, tequila, mint, plums
sour	yuzu	true sour citrus	juice, infuse, muddle, liqueur	apricots, carrots, gin, ginger, grapefruit, lemon, mango, oranges, vodka
sour	cranberries	true sour non-citrus	juice, infuse, liqueur, puree	amaretto, apples, cinnamon, Cognac, brandy, vodka, gin, ginger, honey, lemon, lime, oranges, triple sec, maple syrup, peaches, pears, pumpkin, vanilla
sour-aromatic	sweet vermouth	slightly sweet	as is	whiskey, bourbon (see their friends for more suggestions)
sour-aromatic	Dubonnet	slightly sweet	as is	whiskey, bourbon (see their friends for more suggestions)
sour-aromatic	dry vermouth	mild tartness	as is	gin, vodka (see their friends for more suggestions)
sour-aromatic	Lillet	slightly sweet	as is	gin, vodka (see their friends for more suggestions)
sour-aromatic	Campari	bitterness	as is	Galliano, grapefruit, orange, pineapple, ginger, lemon, vodka
sour-aromatic	Cynar	bitterness	as is	orange, vermouth, grapefruit
sour-aromatic	amaro	bitterness	as is	strawberries, orange, vodka, brandy

The Flavor Profile Chart

Category	Ingredient	Other Characteristics	Method to Make It Cocktail-Ready	Friends
sour-herbal	cilantro	mild sweetness	muddle	cucumbers, ginger, lemons, limes, mint, oranges, mango. *Foes:* whiskey, bourbon, scotch, brandy, applejack/calvados
sour-spice	ginger	aromatic	infuse, syrup, muddle, liqueur	apples, apricots, basil, bell peppers, cilantro, coconut, cranberries, figs, grapefruit, lemon, lime, guava, honey, kumquats, lavender, lychee, mango, melon, mint, papaya, passion fruit, pears, plums, pumpkin, raspberries, rhubarb, vanilla
sour-sweet	blackberries	mild sweetness	syrup, muddle, infuse, liqueur	apricots, bananas, apples, brandy, triple sec, honey, lemon, lime, mango, melon, mint, nectarines, peaches, oranges, raspberries, strawberries, vanilla, watermelon
sour-sweet	blueberries	mild sweetness	syrup, muddle, infuse, liqueur	apricots, bananas, blackberries, Cognac, honey, lemon, lime, triple sec, mangoes, mint, nectarines, peaches, pears, raspberries, rhubarb, watermelon
sour-sweet	pomegranate	mild sweetness	syrup, infuse, liqueur	bananas, cinnamon, coconut, cucumber, ginger, grapefruit, honey, kumquat, lemon, lime, oranges, tequila, gin, vodka
sour-sweet	tomatoes	mild sweetness	juice, muddle, infuse	basil, gin, vodka, tequila, bell peppers, cilantro, cucumbers, fennel, ginger, honey, lavender, lemon, lime, mango, mint, oranges, pineapple, rosemary, strawberries, watermelon
sweet	almonds	slightly savory	syrup (orgeat), liqueur (amaretto)	brandy, Champagne, cherries, Cognac, falernum, figs, lemon, lime, maraschino liqueur, peaches, pears, rum, triple sec
sweet	apples	mild tartness	juice, infuse	cinnamon, applejack/calvados, whiskey, lemon, rum, ginger, vanilla, Cognac, honey, triple sec, vodka
sweet	apricots	light	syrup, puree, muddle, infuse	apples, apricot brandy, brandy, scotch, blackberries, blueberries, cherries, cinnamon, Cognac, cranberries, lemon, honey, oranges, peaches, raspberries, rosemary, strawberries, triple sec
sweet	bananas	mild tartness	infuse, blended drinks, liqueur	blueberries, blackberries, brandy, Cognac, applejack/calvados, cinnamon, coconut, coffee liqueur, honey, guava, lemon, lime, mango, papaya, pineapple, rum, raspberries, pomegranate, strawberries, vanilla
sweet	bell peppers (yellow, orange, red)	mild bitterness	muddle, infuse	basil, cilantro, ginger, honey, lemon, gin, vodka, lime, mint, tomatoes

The Flavor Profile Chart

Category	Ingredient	Other Characteristics	Method to Make It Cocktail-Ready	Friends
sweet	blackberries (wild)	mild tartness	syrup, muddle, infuse, liqueur	tequila, gin, mint, basil, lemon, lime, orange, bourbon, whiskey, cherries, apricots, peaches, pineapple
sweet	cantaloupe	light	puree, muddle	basil, ginger, grapefruit, lemon, lime, other melons, watermelon, mint, raspberries, Champagne
sweet	carrots	soft herbal	juice	apples, basil, gin, vodka, ginger, cinnamon, lemon, lime, orange, triple sec
sweet	cherries	mild tartness	muddle, infuse, liqueur, syrup	apricots, brandy, Cognac, whiskey, bourbon, cinnamon, figs, honey, lemon, lime, triple sec, nectarines, oranges, peaches, plums, raspberries, vanilla, vodka
sweet	cinnamon	spiced	syrup, infuse	figs, honey, peaches, maple syrup, vodka, whiskey, bourbon, scotch, pears, pineapples
sweet	coconut	strong sweetness	infuse, liqueur, cream puree	bananas, basil, cilantro, grapefruit, guava, lemon, lime, kiwi, mangoes, oranges, papaya, passion fruit, pineapple, vanilla, strawberries
sweet	cucumber	mild tartness	muddle, infuse	bell peppers, cilantro, gin, vodka, lemon, lime, melon, watermelon, pineapple, tomatoes
sweet	figs	mild tartness	syrup, infuse	orgeat, amaretto, apples, cherries, cinnamon, ginger, grapes, honey, lavender, lemon, lime, raspberries, mangoes, mint, oranges, pears, vanilla
sweet	grapes	occasionally tart	juice, syrup, muddle	apples, brandy, Cognac, honey, mint, lemon, pears, cranberries, raspberries, strawberries
sweet	guava	light	juice, syrup, puree, muddle	bananas, coconut, ginger, honey, lemon, lime, oranges, passion fruit, pineapple, strawberries, rum, vanilla
sweet	honey	floral	syrup, liqueur	amaretto, apples, apricots, bananas, brandy, Cognac, cinnamon, coconut, coffee liqueur, red currants, ginger, grapefruit, guava, kiwi, kumquats, lemon, lime, oranges, lavender, lychee, melon, mint, papaya, peaches, pears, persimmons, plum, pomegranate, pumpkin, rum, rhubarb, tequila, vanilla, whiskey, bourbon, gin, vodka, applejack/calvados
sweet	honeydew	light	puree, muddle	basil, blackberries, Champagne, figs, ginger, grapefruit, honey, lemon, lime, melons, mint, nectarines, peaches, strawberries
sweet	lychees	true sweet	muddle, infuse, liqueur, syrup, puree	blackberries, blueberries, strawberries, ginger, melon, kiwi, lemon, lime, mangoes, oranges, tangerines, pears, pineapples, plum, rum, vodka, raspberries

The Flavor Profile Chart

Category	Ingredient	Other Characteristics	Method to Make It Cocktail-Ready	Friends
sweet	mangoes	true sweet	muddle, infuse, liqueur, syrup, puree	bananas, bell peppers, cilantro, blackberries, blueberries, strawberries, rum, vodka, pisco, Champagne, cinnamon, coconut, ginger, grapefruit, honey, kiwi, kumquat, lemon, lime, mint, oranges, triple sec, pineapple, passion fruit, papaya, raspberries, strawberries, vanilla, vodka, basil
sweet	maple syrup	mild bitterness	as is	bananas, apples, apricots, blueberries, whiskey, bourbon, cinnamon, figs, ginger, lemon, lime, nectarines, peaches, oranges, persimmons, plums, pumpkin, strawberries, raspberries, rum, vanilla
sweet	nectarines	true sweet	muddle, syrup, infuse, puree	apricots, blackberries, blueberries, strawberries, oranges, lemon, lime, cherries, Champagne, vodka, ginger, figs, maple syrup, mint, brandy, triple sec, peaches, plums, raspberries, vanilla
sweet	papaya	slightly savory	puree, syrup	bananas, cilantro, lemon, lime, oranges, ginger, grapefruit, kiwi, honey, mango, melon, mint, nectarine, peaches, passion fruit, raspberries, strawberries, vanilla, pineapple
sweet	passion fruit	occasionally tart	puree, syrup	bananas, cilantro, lemon, lime, oranges, triple sec, ginger, kiwi, mangoes, peaches, papayas, pears, pineapples, tangerine, rum, strawberries, tequila
sweet	peaches	true sweet	puree, syrup, muddle, infuse, liqueur	amaretto, apples, apricots, basil, blueberries, Champagne, whiskey, bourbon, blackberries, brandy, rum, applejack/calvados, cherries, cinnamon, Cognac, triple sec, red currants, figs, ginger, honey, lavender, mint, lemon, lime, orange, nectarines, oranges, rum, papaya, passion fruit, pineapple, plums, raspberries, strawberries, vanilla
sweet	pears	true sweet	syrup, infuse, liqueur	amaretto, apples, apricots, bourbon, basil, blackberries, blueberries, brandy, whiskey, applejack/calvados, Champagne, cherries, cinnamon, cranberries, figs, ginger, fennel, triple sec, honey, lemon, lime, oranges, maple syrup, mint, passion fruit, plums, rhubarb, rosemary, rum, vanilla,
sweet	pineapples	mild tartness	syrup, muddle, infuse, liqueur, juice	apricots, bananas, basil, brandy, rum, cilantro, cinnamon, coconut, triple sec, Cognac, ginger, grapefruit, lemon, lime, oranges, honey, kiwi, kumquat, mangoes, mint, papaya, passion fruit, pomegranate, strawberries

The Flavor Profile Chart

Category	Ingredient	Other Characteristics	Method to Make It Cocktail-Ready	Friends
sweet	plums	mild tartness	muddle, syrup, infuse, puree	apricots, brandy, cherries, cinnamon, gin, ginger, honey, lavender, nectarines, peaches, mint, oranges, lemon, lime, raspberries, rum, strawberries, vanilla, whiskey
sweet	strawberries	mild tartness	syrup, muddle, infuse, liqueur, puree	amaretto, apricots, bananas, blackberries, raspberries, blueberries, brandy, tequila, rum, gin, vodka, Champagne, Chartreuse, cinnamon, chocolate, Cognac, elderflower, ginger, grapes, grapefruit, guava, kiwi, lemon, lime, oranges, mangoes, melon, mint, pineapple, plums, pomegranate, rhubarb, vanilla
sweet	tangerines	moderately tart	juice, muddle, infuse, liqueur	apricots, bananas, Campari, triple sec, ginger, honey, lavender, lemon, lime, grapefruit, melon, mint, passion fruit, raspberries, pomegranate
sweet	vanilla	true sweet	syrup, infuse, liqueur	apples, apricots, brandy, chocolate, figs cherries, ginger, honey, lavender, lemon, mint, oranges, peaches, pears, plums, rhubarb, strawberries, tomatoes, whiskey, bourbon, scotch
sweet	watermelon	light	muddle, juice, puree, infuse	basil, mint, blackberries, blueberries, cilantro, fennel, lemon, lime, oranges, melon, pomegranate, raspberries, tequila, vodka
sweet-herbal	basil	aromatic	muddle, syrup, infuse	strawberries, raspberries, blueberries, blackberries, coconut, cucumber, lemon, lime, mint, nectarines, orange, peaches, watermelon, vodka, gin
sweet-herbal	fennel	aromatic	muddle, infuse	apples, bell peppers, ginger, honey, lemon, lime, mint, orange, pears, tomatoes, watermelon
sweet-herbal	lavender	aromatic	syrup, infuse, muddle	apples, amaretto, blackberries, blueberries, cherries, figs, ginger, honey, mint, oranges, peaches, plums, pears, raspberries, strawberries, vanilla, tangerines
sweet-herbal	mint	aromatic	muddle, infuse, syrup, liqueur	*Everything!*
sweet-sour	kiwi	mild sweetness	puree, muddle	bananas, strawberries, blackberries, coconut, grapefruit, honey, lemon, lime, lychee, oranges, mangoes, papaya, pineapple, passion fruit, vodka, rum
sweet-sour	raspberries	mild tartness	syrup, muddle, infuse, liqueur	apricots, blackberries, blueberries, strawberries, brandy, vodka, Champagne, Cognac, triple sec, figs, grapes, grapefruit, honey, lemon, lime, oranges, melon, peaches, pears, pineapple, plum, rhubarb, rum

About the Authors

MARCIA SIMMONS is contributing editor of DrinkoftheWeek.com and editor-in-chief of Liqurious.com, a visual gallery of cocktail indulgences. Her pantry is always filled with bottles and jars of homemade infusions and liqueurs. She's been a professional writer for more than ten years and a professional drinker since 2008.

JONAS HALPREN is the founder and editor of DrinkoftheWeek.com. He started the site in 1999 to share his passion for fine spirits and knowledge of bartending in an accessible way. His goal was to provide creative alternatives to boring cocktails and demystify the intimidating cocktail world for regular folk.

Index